SEASONS AND STREAMS

A BOOK FOR ALL CHAPTERS (SEASONS) OF YOUR LIFE

Katrina Soulshine

Seven Celestials Publishing

ISBN: 978-1-3999-4053-5

Original cover design Katrina Campbell

Digital illustration Tarn Ellis

Contents

Dedication

This book is dedicated to my beautiful daughters, you inspire me and I love you infinitely.

I hope I inspire you - not to be perfect, but to be the truest version of you, moment to moment to moment in this lifetime. To find the wonder in it all and know that you are always held by the Most High.

To my parents, whose love and passion at the time intertwined, when all the elements combined and aligned resulting in the divine spark of life. A cosmic creation destined to come to fruition through the portal of my mother's womb.

I also dedicate this to everyone who has had a hand in raising me, I am so grateful.

With acknowledgment to all who I have encountered on this journey so far and for those I am yet to meet.

Thank you for sharing this path, for being my mirror.

Seasons and Streams – A collection of poetry and prose for all chapters, or seasons, of your life

An Unrefined Stream

Seasons and Cycles

Seasons and streams

Her, she, me

Not too deep, complex or contrived, all her words, from her soul, organic, unrefined

Poetry, Prose, reflections and streams of consciousness

Transmuting pain into poems and power

Prophetic dreams do come true

Seven, seven, seven

A celebration of the multifaceted woman and her reflection in all of nature

You see, when you look to nature you will observe that everything moves in cycles and everything has its season. We as hue- mans have our own seasons, that is evident in the menstrual cycle of a womban, going from spring to summer then into her autumn and winter. Men go through their own cycles. It is when we truly honour the phases of them all, that the transition from one to the next becomes easier.

This book captures the essence of life, the waves we tread as we navigate both the sunshine and the storms.

It is somewhat of a chrysalis…

Transformation in motion, transmutation, splitting open

Unfolding into freedom.

Like a lotus

Inspired by me, inspired by you, inspired by life.

Us

Earthing

Ascending

A modern-day word weaver, the codes are in my captions

The writing is on the wall

An unrefined soul finding her way home…

Multidimensional soul codes

Multidimensional downloads

Intuitive soul muse decoding mysteries

Words infused with potent frequency

Tap into whichever mood you embody and transmute your energy

Word alchemy

Uninhibited expression

Words on love, heartbreak, healing, joy, race, spirituality, divinity and awakening

Life.

Introduction

It was 2005 …warm sand beneath our feet, the gentle Trade wind breeze intermittently kissing our cheeks as we strolled along the beach.

I recall the pale blue cotton shirt of the man who appeared seemingly out of nowhere, the top two buttons left undone. I guess that was his way of counteracting the relentless heat.

His demeanour was polite and his smile welcoming as he approached my mother and me. On British soil he would be considered a stranger, but on Bajan sands, an old friend.

First, he shook my mother's hand, then when it came to shaking mine, he held on to it that little bit longer. My first inclination was to pull it away, and no sooner than that thought entered my head, these words left his mouth -

"ahhhh, you, you're a writer, you have ink in your veins".

A chance encounter on that island in 2005 stayed at home with me, in my heart, till this day. Almost twenty years after that moment and with insights into past lives since then, I birth this book. Written in the fleeting moments between doing and being. Working, adventuring, healing and parenting during a pandemic. Bigger still, a monumental shift in the consciousness and standing of humanity.

The stars and sunrise always consistent company. Late nights, early risings, comforted largely by the soft warm glow of my Himalayan salt lamp and the flicker of my favourite candle. Binaural beats or nostalgic tunes in my headphones beset against the faint scent of my favourite natural incense, evoking memories and emotions.

There have been times I have forgotten my power, dimmed my light, been told I'm too deep, silenced. But sometimes it takes the eyes of another to reflect back to you, the magic you behold.

You are a radiant cosmonaut transmitting codes from many dimensions through your cosmic higher self. These codes are creations that you birth which are visual activations woven into artistry. Your crown is flowing with streams of information that feel like solar rays gently infusing with your creative centres as you bring forward ascension guidance and your own very ancient wisdom.

There are layers of your Akash that are opening and revealing new memories or gifts that are connected to a past lifetime working as a cocoa Shaman who created sacred elixir and infused it with magical chants and incantations that was given to the community.

You also downloaded lots of images which were prophetic, when in a trance and you wove these images onto a form of fabric through a wooden loom to create patchwork blankets which told the story of your community.

An aspect of you comes forward, she is midnight blue with rippling waves of royal blue hair. She is holding two orbs, one in each hand and she rolls them out towards the earth.

These orbs land in your (present self) hands and you integrate them as they are part of your cosmic toolkit regarding healing. The orbs connect you to the wisdom from all your lifetimes and your ancestral lines. You feel deeply the rhythm and tides of energy upon the planet as they swirl into motion and create waves which you swim through and relate through your words.

You are able to translate the experience of energy.

There is much balance and harmony now occurring within you as the inner child is nurtured by the inner parents who support one another in their unified masculine and feminine energy. After the Equinox vibrations peak you are gifted more opportunities to create from that unified space within and bring into your life reflections of your heart through your connections and your own artistic creations. Your Higher Self is wearing her crown and channelling the universal wisdom through it to you and you can guide others with your vision and wisdom (insights by @blueroseoraclesxx -March 2021)

I have been told my words carry healing codes, and to me that is magical, because healing is my passion and a huge part of my purpose. I have connected more deeply to myself through embarking on this healing journey. I hold space for myself through my exploration of words and I connect with others in sharing them.

Counting my blessings, noting the lessons, from it all. Secrets, tears, revelations, laughter. Bereavement, trauma and joy. Self-care, self-discovery, the revolution and therapy through various healing modalities, all of it is woven throughout what I write.

This is a book reflecting on the seasons of life, the cycles, chapters and journeys. Arrival at a place of knowing, only to discover that you know nothing at all, before embarking onward to the next destination. The North Star as your guiding light.

I like to think of the analogy of a huge train stain, kind of like Clapham Junction. There are many intermingling tracks and with a flick of a switch, you might change the course of your route, however the destination will always remain the same.

The destination is your destiny.

One of the key aspects of my awakening has been through the acknowledgment and honour of my genealogy.

It was in recent years that I learned that 95% of your DNA comes from your mother.

When we look to Mother Nature, we see the reflection of women, cyclical in rhythms, elemental, nurturing, brutal, and all that is in between.

For centuries, women have been silenced, vilified, persecuted for simply speaking their truth and sharing their innate powers. It is clear to me as I grow in age and remember my innate wisdom, that this is because our power has always been known and it's intimidating to those who know they cannot contain nor control it.

Honouring your genetic inheritance is a huge key to the self-love and in- powerment journey (and yes, I wrote in-powerment rather than empowerment). It was when I changed the language and perspective from referring to certain aspects of my ancestral inheritance and healing as being a burden, to acknowledging the triumph and power that my ancestors beheld in order for me to be right here, right now, that my paradigm shifted.

This book delves deep into the nuance of rediscovery, reawakening and rebirth.

There is a Chinese proverb which reads, "When sleeping women awake, mountains will move" and ***womban*** does it feel like mountains are moving at an accelerated pace.

We are at the dawn of an ancient new age.

A remembrance.

As I type, it feels like the baby is in the birth canal being gently urged by the rhythmical surges of labour, ready to crown.

Womban, is on the ascent back to her rightful place and she will be seen, she will be heard, and she will be respected.

And any man in his divinity will observe and respect that fact because he knows that this is the age of the universal scales being tipped back into balance.

Be You to the Full

...because all they'll see is the cover

and yes they'll make assumptions of the author

but they won't know the creative process

nor the blood, sweat and tears

the emotions that inspired the story

the revisions to each version

so, it is not your job as the author to worry about their review of the book, just as long as you are happy with the words

because the truth of the matter is, one million people could lay eyes on your journey

but not one person sees the world exactly as you do

and with that in mind

continue to do you and be you

to the full

CHAPTER 1
ANCESTRAL WISDOM

Not Just For a Season

Not just for a season
Nor a day
But for thousands of lifetimes
Not for a patriarchal appointed month

In my quest for knowledge of my ancestry I discovered that Africa and South America hold wealth beyond our wildest dreams
In its people and in its properties
And by the latter, I don't the mean bricks and mortar you have been led to believe as true value
But in the gold, bauxite, diamonds, cocoa and more
Lands holding wealth that made the western world lustful in its quest to dominate and rape

I learned that black women hold mitochondrial DNA that encompasses every race
Let that sink in
That's power
Is it any wonder then that black women have been the most oppressed and silenced in history?
And there is a reason black woman hold so much power, as do our black men
It's written in the very fibre of our DNA and guess what
The fallen oppressors knew that
It is why for a number of lifetimes they have tried to remove her, she, I, *me* from what comes naturally
From a connection to ourselves and therefore our connection to our great mother Earth
We are bright like the sun,
Rich brown like the soil
Golden like the autumn leaves
Our dark coiled hair holds power like an electricity you cannot fathom
Crowned in all our glory
But somehow they managed to wipe our memories
Made us forget
To be enslaved to a narrative not befitting of our true majesty

To distract generation after generation with promises of lifestyles that harm us
But we hear the call of the whispers of our ancestral angels
Reminders of the secrets that laid dormant for some time
Now being activated with a remembering, an unlearning and a relearning
Not just for a day, nor a month, but for all eternity.

Honour to the Ancestors

Feelings of remembrance and absolute love to any of my ancestors who were made to feel less than they were, as a result of displacement and falsehoods. I rescind any agreement they knowingly or unknowingly entered into with false institutions

I reclaim their peace and their power on their behalf. They kept going and provided so much and for that I am eternally grateful

Can you imagine the volumes of untold stories that lay within the hearts of your loved ones?

I can…

Do not focus on the detractors and the distractions because that could ultimately lead you to your destruction.

His Story

You taught me about King Henry VIII

And Alexander the Great

But why did you not school me about Queen Califia

Or the Egyptian Goddesses Isis and Ma'at?

You told me about Augustus, but failed to mention Queen Amanirenas

It was she, leader of the Kushites who stood against Rome defending the Nile

The *original* Queen Mothers

Great dynasties of times gone by

It was the man in the market that told me that the true story is told through the lens of another eye

There is so much more to know as these secrets are unearthed

And all of those hidden stories and truths will surely come to light as we usher in the ancient new earth

You are the Queen of your own domain, powerful and protected, listen within.

Giza

The scale of the pyramids taught me this
you know much, yet you know nothing at all
so you might as well get comfortable accepting that you will never know it all

There is nothing like the intuition of a woman, especially one carrying the future or recently having given birth to it.

Sleeping Lions
You saw in me what I had yet to see
That is why whilst I was praying
You were preying
Lurking in the shadows like a ravenous hyena
But you know what happens when you poke a sleeping lion one too many times
She awakens
And it is then that you will come to realise that her bite
Is far more dangerous than your bark

Decolonise my mind
I love it when you talk to me of my ancestors
The sun, moon and the stars
I see constellations when you speak of our ancient nations
Every word you speak, so powerful
reminding me of exactly who we are

Your lessons move the cogs in my mind
turning everything I once knew on its head
I lose all sense of (Gregorian) time
I get the tingles down my spine
Your willing student, so eager to learn
I would let you decolonise my mind any time

To the Ancestors

I am eternally grateful for you, for without you, there would be no me.

The Call

…and it was then, in that ultimate moment of surrender that they came to me. They told me - "it is time" that I must answer the call

that I must do the job.

In hindsight they'd been telling me that for all of my life

They showed me it all

And I felt it all

The sadness, the sorrow, the shock, the love, the power, the loss

My cells transported through lifetimes, upon lifetimes, upon lifetimes

Shaking my head and clutching my heart

On my knees, I wept

"But it is so hard, it's so so hard" my inner child self pleading

"Please don't leave me, please *please* don't leave me I need you!"

Both gently and firmly they replied

"No"

"It is you and it is time; *you* have the strength to do it and this is why we chose you"

Nodding through tears of resistance and pain I cried

Sobbing what felt like a river and over time, the intensity lessened, and I felt held

Truth is, they never left me, they never will

Calmly, they handed it to me, and so, I took it

Crowned

An in that moment I told myself through the longing and sadness

I know I have to do it

And so I'll do it

I WILL do it

I'm a little scared but I promise you I'll do it

And so I did it

And it is done

And so it is

Ancestors, I see you, I feel you, I honour you, I thank you, I love you.

Abundant freedom, prosperity, peace and power is ours, now and forever, and so it is.

Your evolution is a revolution.

Where are you *really* from?

When they ask me I stammer over the answer
"What do you mean where am I from?" Is what I wish to reply
But If you really must know
I am from the stars that cover your head each night
The sun which makes every living thing flourish
I am from the mountainous lush green hills
The clay that sustains your village
The gold mined deep in the rivers
The waterfalls wild and free
The precious gems they lust for
The cacao they water down
The moon that illuminates all when the cycle comes around
So if you really must know, I am from everywhere and nowhere

Brown Sugar

Sugar

Not the bleached and refined kind you find on the shelf of a supermarket floor

The unrefined and natural kind

The one that grows directly in the fields of fertile foreign lands

Caressed by the heavy humid breeze

Abundantly

Growing wild and free

Towards the sun

Infinitely

Organic

That kind

Sugar

Soul Ties

Is it any wonder I'm confused?
My soul is tied to three continents
Where should my loyalty lie?
Don't ask me!
One of the continents I am yet to truly see
So therefore, I really am yet to decide, what home truly means to me

Back Home

What does home mean to you?

Home is the fish and chip shop on the high street

The forests and fields of green

It's a distant memory of Africa

Earth tones and mountain streams

It's the bustling streets of London town

But a longing to be elsewhere

Its sitting under a palm tree on the golden sand, no worries, no cares

Lost in Translation

The Mother tongue
She speaks to me in a way in which only she can
It is received just how it is meant to feel
With connection
With nuance
With love

Stripped

Of my name
Of my language
Of my healing
Of my land
Of my story
Stripped
Barren
Bare

The captor will never truly educate their captives.

Rebuilding an Empire

They tore down your walls, they ripped off your crown

They ridiculed your teachings and tried to hide what you wrote down

But your story was written in the planets and stars

The time has come around and the victory will be ours

Awaken all of you, you know just who you are

For the time has now come and the victory is ours.

Heritage

I envisage how the invisible thread of heritage is passed from generation to generation

Intricately woven tales creating a beautiful and unique piece of tapestry

Each strand connecting one to the other for all eternity

Indigenous

I wonder if the indigenous tribes are laughing at us now?
Ripped from their lands
Blood on his hands
Mocked for their traditions
They honour the earth, whilst we destroy it
But yet we call *them* savage
Riches stolen, claimed by thieves
Immeasurable damage
I wonder if they know of our masks
Human separation
Of fines and trickery
Of roads and doorways blocked like rat runs
of unnatural “remedies”
I wonder if they mock us now or weep tears of empathy
Do you ever wonder of such things, or is it only me?

Words are swords and swords are dangerous, but they are also defence and protection. Words cast spells, so when you cast your net, be conscious of what it is you wish to catch.

Guidance (936hz)

God, Source, Angels, Guides
Higher self, soul
Continue to lead the way
I am open to the path that aligns with my highest timeline
I will walk this path with faith, hope and love
Pausing only to give gratitude for your reverence
Guide me
Guide me
Guide me
All the way home

Seven Miles of Silence

Sisters walking in silent solidarity
strangers but strangely familiar
scaling an unknown territory
confidently reclaiming peace
taking up space
not a sound
yet speaking volumes
passers-by wonder
as we wander
home away from home
finding home within our bones
sisters
walking in silent solidarity
scaling an unknown territory
confidently reclaiming our peace

I am free and I hold all of the answers within. I am soul sovereign.

Revolutions and Revelations

Where there is a wheel, where there is your will

If it is divine will

There will always be a way

Soul Rebel

When you captured my body and tore away my child

You broke my heart and fractured my soul

The fruits of my womb in your eyes, merely a product of labour

Night after night I wept into the darkness

Until suddenly, the tears were no more

As the sun rose and light pierced through the cracks of the tomb

I made a silent agreement

The violation would never happen again

And that promise crossed continents

That covenant spanned lifetimes

It trickled like hushed whispers from generation to generation

Falling upon those with ears to hear

Until it landed with this one particular soul who refused to stay silent

She screamed that promise so loud that it ripped a hole in the ethers

Travelling across dimension and timelines

Rousing the lips of the one who first uttered those very same words

Until simultaneously, in unison, without ever having met

They both expressed

"Not in this lifetime"

Our foremothers and forefathers honoured the wisdom of nature, rather than factory farm their desired outcomes, they would watch the weather for signs, honour the natural cycle of seasons and they looked to the sky for guidance. It was in the stars that they tracked their way to far off destinations and by the rising and setting of the sun by which they strategically designed great monuments that would long outlive their time on this earth…

CHAPTER 2
AUTUMN

Notes on Autumn...

I adore her, I welcome her with open arms. Perhaps being an autumn baby has a lot to do with it. It is the opportunity to return back into the womb, to hibernate

Maybe procreate, be that babies or ideas! Letting them marinate slowly in gestation.

It is permission to hide away...to fall into her darkness is to trust and surrender.

Nothing excites me more than the golden hues of leaves that have fallen to the ground. The sound of them under my feet.

The crisp air

The most beautiful sunrise skies.

The opportunity to give thanks for shelter as the cold nights draw in, fireworks, tight warm hugs, cocoa, cinnamon, nutmeg, ginger and cloves.

I think of the seasons as trimesters like the stages of pregnancy. Autumn is where the seed is sown...the epitome of divine mother

She honours her rest and preserves her energy to give birth to beautiful new blooms in the months ahead.

She's naked stripped bare to her roots, nothing to hide. Nothing to lose. Everything to look forward to, she just is...

Dark Night of The Soul - Shadow Work

There is no way to escape the shadow

least not in the light

he or she is always there

until you do the work

Harvest

Do you dare to bury the seeds of your desires into the darkest depths of the soil, trusting that through the alchemy of the elements, and in that time of silent gestation in the womb of the earth, that every single one will bear the living fruits of your loving labour,

no poking

no prodding

no scanning

just silence

and trust

Hibernation

The darker nights are like permission to hide away

To step into the darkness

To trust the stillness in the silence

To surrender in order to die, to be reborn.

Shedding

Letting you go was what taught
me the truest form of love

If you knew that everything you desire is already on its way, what would you do differently in this moment?

Words Are Spells

If I could cast spells there would be no limit to what I would do
Dance around the sun
Fly around the moon
Simultaneously climb all the mountain peaks
Envision and bring to life the highest timeline for you and for me
But you see
There is no "if"
Because what you can conceive has, is and will always be
We are all magicians
You just didn't realise that the spell was the veil concealing you from the multiverse within
Made you think it was a sin just so you couldn't win
But consciousness is key
Once you attain that you will truly see you hold all the power, what you want wants you
Abracadabra
And so mote it be

Release

For Autumn has no attachments
she simply smiles
releasing with ease
knowing that what is for her
will return in the springtime.

The seeds I am sowing now are cultivating the most abundant harvest.

Autumn Equinox

like the moon, the tides, seasons and cycles, they've come back around right when needed, like a memorable teacher, in divine timing

The moon was bright and the air was still. The universal balance was found, much release took place...it was needed.

Autumn to me is the epitome of the divine mother, I adore her, I welcome her with open arms. Perhaps being an autumn baby has a lot to do with it. It's the opportunity to return back into the womb, to hibernate- maybe procreate - be that babies or ideas!
Letting them marinate slowly.

It's permission to hide away
To fall into her darkness is to trust and surrender.

Nothing excites me more than the golden hues of leaves that have fallen to the ground
The sound of them under my feet.
The crisp air
The most beautiful sunrise skies
The opportunity to give thanks for shelter as the cold nights draw in
Fireworks
Tight warm hugs
cocoa, cinnamon, nutmeg, ginger, cloves ...

I think of the seasons as trimesters like the stages of pregnancy
Autumn is where the seed is sown

Autumn is the epitome of divine mother

She honours her rest and preserves her energy to give birth to beautiful new blooms in the months ahead
She's naked, stripped bare to her roots, nothing to hide
She just is.

I don't agree with the concept of not grieving as it says in one of these images, do grieve what has fallen away if that's what comes, make room for it all. Welcome grief with loving arms and when you feel ready, let it go...

And once the grieving has subsided, make way for acceptance, with love
in the knowing, that what is for you, will always return in the springtime.

The rest is sometimes more important than the work.

Exhale

It is only when you are gone that I can put down my shield
Let down my guard
The protector rests her armour
Sinks into her pillow
Closes her eyes
Pours out her heart
And allows the tears to flow
And flow they do
Freely
Deep release
These tears, they carry love, they carry heartbreak, they carry grief
But oh, the wave of peace that comes, when I allow myself to release

First Frost

I love it when the early risings are bathed in sunshine
Those moments where I can take my time
To get totally lost in my mind
Inside
First frost under my feet
Birdsong serenading me

Use Me as Your Instrument

Use me, I am yours
An empty vessel
Pluck my strings softly
Make a melody
turn it into a symphony

Fall

Autumn

A time to slow down after an abundantly shiny, fast paced summer

To set and sow seeds of intention

To witness the slow sway of leaves as they dance to the floor beneath

Bearing witness to the naked branches showing powerful vulnerability in all of their glory

The glorious orange and golden hues that encapsulated the sun now a regal blanket beneath your feet on the forest floor

A golden magical carpet leading you home

Autumn feels like the foetal position you took in your first home

Perhaps you spoon yourself or your love

Where two wholes join souls and quantumly merge to become one

A perfect paradox

This seasonal equinox

Where x marks the spot

And both hemispheres receive equal light

No need to tussle or fight

Balance

Naked Woman

Naked woman
Stripped bare like a tree in autumn.
The winds revealing all of me, all of she
Femininity
Sexuality
Perfection
Imperfections
Unique
Signature
One of one
Second to none
Naked woman

37

The year that tested my commitment to myself
would I stand my ground and own my throne
or would I revert back to the obedient little girl
questioning my voice and my knowing.
At times it felt like everyone left me
or perhaps it was I who left everyone
there were moments we weft in and out
like the trade winds
or the waves as they kiss the shore
but I realised that my compass was internal
and my heart said “due north”
so off I embarked on what was later revealed to me
as
The Hero's Journey …

CHAPTER 3
WINTER

Cold Shoulders, Cold Shores

Cold shoulders, Cold shores
I can only imagine the hardships endured
"No dogs, no Irish, no blacks"
You'd made your voyage now, too late to turn back
Determined and resilient, you swallowed your pride "Wog"
"Darkie" "Coon", your majesty, denied.
As you walked through its narrow cobbled streets, you often pondered -
You spoke the "mother tongue " this was the mother country,
"why turn your back on me now, when it was you who had called me?" You fought for her freedom, you defended her land, but this experience was a bitter contradiction, so hard to understand.

They questioned your hygiene and looked down at your attire.
But you came from sunshine and colour, it was them who lived in grey, dirty squalor, in some parts it was a quagmire.
Qualified and upstanding from whence you came, just to be told your papers meant nothing, looked down on with disdain.
This move was just temporary, you had come to achieve clear goals, bracing the chill daily was your only resolve.

You laid down your roots and sowed generations of seeds...product of which, beautiful brown boys, girls women and men, just like me.

I can only imagine the hardships you endured, when you embarked on that journey only to be met with cold shoulders, cold shores.

Full Moon

It is deep and it is shallow
Its complex and simplicity
Light and dark
Fire and ice
It's textured
Its warm
It will envelope you and hold you tight
Embrace it all

Moonwalk

The sun tips his hat and bows out as she enters the room
Big
Bright
Full moon
She could blind you with her aura
Sometimes she's bashful and she hides behind the clouds
Other times she's bold as brass and makes her presence felt
Loud and proud
For she knows that whilst the sun guides the planets
She guides both the time and tides
She'll take you home with her magnetic grip
An unavoidable gravitational pull
Pull you in, push you out
Make your waves rise and then fall
Once a month she comes out to play adorned with an aura of love
What a blessing this queen of the night
Always watching you from above
Just one look into her sphere and she'll have you bursting to the brim
With magic

Stripped

Sometimes we need to take it even further back than the roots, stripped further, to the soil, to the seed.

Barren

She sits by the window watching the snowflakes fall upon the empty Common

reminiscing of summer days gone by

“Is it 1975?” She asks, her purse at the ready, awaiting the date with the love of her life

What she doesn’t realise is that it is almost 37 years that have since passed

That’s four hundred and forty-four months

13,414 days

And 324,336 hours

“no its not” is all I could reply with a loving smile as the snowflakes continued to fall

One by one

“its not 1975”

I am exactly where I am supposed to be or else I simply wouldn't be here.

Remember Who You Are

If you are raised by people who do not know who they are

How can they possibly teach you who you are?

Then you spend hours upon hours

Days upon days

Entangled with institutions who make it their job to ensure you dare not find out the truth of who you are

It comes to a point in time when the onus is on you

To remember

To remember

To remember

Remember

Who

You

Are

Fated Encounters with Venus

The space had been calling me for some weeks
I heard the whispers
I felt the pull
But until now, the stars had not aligned
However
On this fateful day, everything and everyone cleared out of my way and I scooped the last ticket, to take my place in such a divinely orchestrated space
Isn't it funny how life goes?
Full circle
All those years ago my mum would drop me off to a summer play-scheme by the block of flats just opposite this same spot
I always felt a little out of place there
Years passed and I returned to that same space for work purposes
To tell people that "the greatest show on Earth" was to be built upon their doorstep
2012
Bulldozing over memories and paving over the cracks with a smile and the promise of free tickets
Fast forward nine years
I got out of my car and looked up, awe-stricken by the stars and moon beset against the backdrop of a clear black sky
Approaching the wooden doors, I knock
There is no answer
A few minutes pass and a car pulls up slowly
My mind wonders if it's some man trying his luck
I roll my eyes and then to my surprise someone steps out of the back passenger side
She walks over
I notice her cherry stained lips and faux fur coat
On the surface we have that in common
A small dog in her hands
We stand side by side and I say "are you going to the event?"
"yeah" she says
"Okay, I am too" I say

A few more silent seconds pass and I offer to her "I'm Katrina, what's your name?"
And in a tone which I can only describe as bittersweet treacle she looks straight into my eyes and replies "Venus"

CHAPTER 4
SPRING

Tree Teachers

Tomorrow go outside and find the nearest tree…look at her, do you think she is looking at you?

She doesn't need anyone outside of her to tell her what to do, how and when to do it, she just does what she does, listening within.

Rooted in her purpose, sure of herself, blooming, blooming, blooming.

Every single day.

When people ask me what inspires me or who I wanna be, my answer will be, if anything, I wanna be more like that tree.

In To Me See

Intimacy sees the mind, it sees the body
and most importantly, it sees the soul

Fertile ground

Sometimes that mess you made turns
out to be the richest fertiliser

Bliss

Open air
Cool breeze
You and me
Natural light
Twilight
Dancing freely under the moonlight
The trees
Nowhere to be but here
Nothing to do but this
The babies running wild and free
Happy as can be
Because that's how it should always be
Safe to roam
To play
To hide and go seek
What is this?
It is pure bliss

Pure

When I told you Katrina means pure, I didn't say it meant perfect.

I am a magnet of love, light and a wealth of great things!

Gestation and Rebirth

At first it felt dark
Quiet
Lonely even
A word unbeknownst to me
But then
I recognised the opportunity
Stillness
Solitude
Growth
Silence
Till one day, the floodgates opened
And before I knew it, I was gently guided along a corridor I hadn't seen before
I didn't know the way, but I trusted the force of nature that was pulling me forth
Towards the end of the canal was a light
I looked back but the path was dark and closed
And so, I continued forward
Closer and closer towards the light I made my way
Until I reached the end
It was show time, go-time
And in that very moment,
I
was
birthed

The Orchid Doesn't Sparkle Anymore

When I welcomed the orchid into my home, I felt happy, she took pride of place

White orchids symbolising elegance

Pink orchids symbolising grace

This orchid, my orchid, the perfect mix of both

But sadly, as the months passed, stunted was her growth

The orchid lost her flowers

Slowly one by one

I tried and tried to revive her, wanting to restore the beauty she once bestowed

But my efforts came to nothing

She was tired

Growing old.

My wishing and willing were seemingly in vain

On much closer inspection, she didn't look the same.

Searching her delicate petals

I sat and I stared

Longingly waiting for that pearlescent shimmer to reappear, but now all that remains in her stem which is bare.

Her radiant glisten is a memory which will stay with me for sure, and memories is all I have

For my orchid doesn't sparkle anymore

Rooted

Yes, your winds might move me and yeah, I may lose a couple leaves but recognise this, my roots are as long and deep as I am tall…come what may, I will not fall.

I trust in the divine timing of my life; I will not compare myself to others.

Lost

Lost
In the stillness
In the silence
In the wonder
In awe
Of it all
Is where you will find me

In The Sand

Some say you shouldn't bury your head in the sand
I say do
Bury your head
Your hands
Your feet
Your heart and soul in the sand
Over and over and over again

Who is She?

She is the epitome of someone rooted in her purpose and blooming beautifully.

She is sowing seeds and creating and creating a legacy, not only for herself, but for many as she grows, that's who.

She stands perfectly imperfect in all her majesty.

Some of her leaves slightly weathered, but that does not detract from the life force that she is.

She is attracting all that aligns with her vision of her highest self.

Continually growing with each new day.

CHAPTER 5
SUMMER

Free

I wanna zip line though the jungle
Dance naked under the moonlight and scream so that my vice
reverberates of off the raindrops on each and every leaf
Lay upon the sunshine
Stare into the stars
Free is where I want to be
And where free is, is never too far

Quiet Storm

She was something like a hurricane, she breezed into my life
Tore down my ego
Stripped me naked
Saw my soul
Took me to a place where there was nowhere to hide
But she saw me
And I saw her
So, I guess you could call it somewhat of a bittersweet destruction

Nectar

The sweet nature of her nectar oozes like molten honey
Once you get a taste it's like sipping the elixir of life
All of your cells will awaken and things will never be the same again

Photosynthesis, is the process by which green plants and certain other organisms transform light energy into chemical. During photosynthesis in green plants, light energy is captured and used to convert water, carbon dioxide, and minerals into oxygen and energy-rich organic compounds.

Photosynthesis in the maintenance of life on the planet. If photosynthesis ceased, there would soon be little food or other organic matter on Earth. Light is life.

Sunshine

You don't always have to wait for the clouds to clear to seek the sun – you are the sun

New Dawn

Rise
Open your eyes
Slowly
Allow your lids to peel back
Like curtains
Draw them open
Let God's daylight in
Remove the sleep
Take in this new vision
A manifestation of your dream come true
New earth
No longer hidden
In full sight
I see you

Flow

I went with the flow and it led me to you

True, Deep, Love

I don't just wanna love you for your flowers
I wanna love you right up from your roots
Without the makeup
Behind the mask
Before the stories
And above the ego
That's the you I want to love...

Frequency

speak to me and I will listen with intent
but honestly
it's not your words I'm reading
it is your frequency that I'm feeling

Forget what anyone else says, follow your heart.

Roots

I often wonder to the roots of my favourite trees
The depths of their stronghold
rooted in majesty and rising year upon year
I wonder what stories they would tell
the seasons they have seen
hidden in the deep dark depths of the shadows
allowing the branches to reach up into the light

Balm

You envelope me
You enrich me
You nurture me
You soothe me
You soften me
Every, single, day

Madam Butterfly

I wonder what madam butterfly thinks as she flirts with the flowers before she ascends

her wings brush upon the clouds as she floats higher and higher

soaring gracefully

captivating everyone who catches sight of her

if she could speak, perhaps she would say a quick hello or a loving goodbye and utter the words “catch me if you can” before making her way to the next destination

observing her teaches us to spread our wings

because you never know which flower you may land upon

Flowers

A flower does not compete with the sun

Coexisting in harmony

They do their thing, naturally understanding that without one, there could not be the other

Celebrating all that they embody, taking their turn to rise and fall

Awaken and rest

Just as mother and father nature, would dictate

Sunrise

Forever may you stop me in my tracks and fill my eyes with light and my heart with love

I found It in the cracks between the clouds

I found it in the cracks between the clouds
They told me we were never lost, we just had to be found
I choose to look up where some might look down
It's profound
The infinite beauty that surrounds us will leave you astounded
Just look at what God did
Shooting stars
Trips to Mars
Profound planetary alignments reminding us who we are
Infinitely limitless
Fractals, not fractured
We were never broken, we were born whole
We are not the body, we are the soul
Are you bold enough to rewrite history
The falsehoods that we have been sold
You are worth far more than your weight in gold
You are the manifestation of the dreams of your ancestors that went untold
And here we are, living breathing
Hearts beating
What a cosmic miracle
Kinda paradoxical
A bittersweet experience
As we seek our deliverance
From the limitations of our mind
For those who dare to seek
Surely they will find
Amongst the cracks
Between the cloud
We were never lost
We just had to be found

Soul song

There is a story in your song

There is a song in your soul

Let it fly free to touch and kiss the hearts and souls of all whom she meets

Let her dance away the sorrow and call upon her joy

There is a story in your song

Don't suppress her

Let her fly

Mya

When I first laid eyes on you, I must admit I wondered if you were an illusion

Was I drowning in my dreams?

The love from my heart spilled over into every single cell of my body

Great mother reborn

A gift to us all

The start of a love that reaches to the stars and beyond

Mya, thank you for the words "drowning in my dreams", evidence of how magnificent you are.

When We Both Grow Up

Who was I to correct her as we lay there on the beach?

The sun shining down on us, beset by the calming sounds of the sea

“I know!” she said, her bright almond eyes beaming back up at me

“We can share shoes mummy, when we both grow up!”

And my heart softened instantly

Admittedly we had spent most of our moments giggling and playing together so freely

So it was no wonder that she perceived me too as a child

The innocence in her bold statement privately amusing me

I love that we connect this way and may the laughter never stop

And yes, my darling we can share shoes

When we both grow up

Soul Rich

my Goals?

My goal isn't for pieces of paper

Or solely for piles of gold

My goal is to stack riches in the heavenly realms of amounts that go untold

I wanna be soul rich that whatever I share is from the overflow

Because I know that anything I spend with good intent comes back to me ten-fold

so yeah, if you want to know what it is that I aim for

It's to stay true to my heart and keep my soul pure

that to me is goals

Antisocial Media

Babe

Don't let an algorithm interfere with your soul's rhythm.

New Kind of Love

What if we were to tear down these walls and rebuild a lifetime

CHAPTER 6
AWAKENING

Do you ever see repeated numbers? It could be 1111, 444, 222 or my favourite for a number of reasons (pun completely intended) - 777.

This could be a sign that you are experiencing a spiritual awakening. Often when we ask for signs, they reveal themselves, and this is not limited to numbers. In addition to numbers, signs appear as animals, colours, scents, songs or that person who calls you the moment you utter their name.

Signs and synchronicities can be witnessed in all things when you realise that those inexplicable occurrences, are not merely coincidence. They are only seen however, when we truly open that higher awareness. When these signs appear, you will have to use discernment, but your intuition will let you know what the signs symbolise in your life.

On my journey, as I have heightened my awareness and deepened my inner knowing, I get perfectly timed triple numbers – also referred to as angel numbers- spirit animals and vivid dreams to name a few! They always arrive when I need confirmation and fuels me to keep on this path and often gives me insights into the next steps to take.

Most of us will be familiar with the phrase "seek and ye shall find" – in essence, you'll often find that when you go in search of something, you will inevitably find it. Where attention goes, energy flows.

Inner Tutor

And how willing are you to trust the innate knowing, even when they come ahead of time and seem crazy?

With all my heart is just how much…

Why?

…because the writing is on the wall

But how do you know?

I don't know how I know, I just know. The writing holds the codes, sort of like braille to a blind person. It is often when we close our eyes that we see the most.

The way that a spire sits atop a church/cathedral, it is the conductor of source intelligence and energy. So too is our crown. I trust my inner spire, my inner tutor, my intuition.

In the light and in the dark, my spirit is my torch and my soul is my guide.

Awakening

I think it's wonderful that a huge amount of the collective is awakening
Questioning the lies that life as we know it has been built upon
Daring to tear that old paradigm down
A moment in time that presents a huge opportunity for us all
This isn't just physical
It's spiritual

01:01

When I realised that what I thought was what I wanted wasn't really what I needed, that is when everything changed

Locked In

When we stay home, we cannot avoid that annoying pile of washing

The seemingly never-ending dishes

The fingerprints

The post

With nowhere to be and nobody to see

It forces us to look in the mirror and see into (face) ourselves

Without the veil of having to be here there and everywhere

Staying home shines a light on the shadows we like to sweep under the rug

And, we could 'flag it' or 'mark as read' and add it to the to do list that might never get done

But really,

With nothing much else to do and time on our side, the time is now- so what are we waiting for?

When

It was almost a year ago that you told me "just two weeks"

But deep in my soul I knew that people such as you are simply characters in a far bigger picture of an abstract painting of which you have very little control.

Over and over again you moved the goal posts dangling a carrot named furlough and free money, but really it is you trying to build an unhealthy co-dependency

Your lies are lost on someone like me and so, after a short while, I listened within, not allowing your gaslighting to stoke up my triggers

I've travelled far and wide within the land of this isle, so for that, I thank you, because without your fallacies and tall stories those adventures might not have been

In that time I have loved and I have lost

Continued to live and learn

I've silenced your noise and turned up my intuition

When you warn me to stay at home and you tried your best to convince me that 1 plus 1 equals 5, I realise that the realest lessons always come from my natural school of thought

I feel sad for those who have fallen for your illusion but I understand they are deeply hypnotised by fear and an age-old programme

You hit me with emotional blackmail and hope I'll surrender

Telling me that if I express human emotion it is akin to murder

I've asked for a year now, if not now, then when?

Over and over and over again

Still awaiting your answer as you maintain this farce

And everyone under your spell is frozen in time

Prisoners of psychological warfare

Unable to see that time moves way too fast

It's a freeing feeling to remove the veil

The way truth and light will always prevail
One life to live in this incarnation
You think you rule me because you preside over a nation
Weill I'm so glad that ultimately, I'm listening to me
One God one life
That's real sovereignty.

2021

Life as you know it, is no more
Some say mother nature has come to settle the score
That it's time to step through a new door
New earth, she beckons
The clock is ticking
Eight minutes, thirty-eight seconds
So, what do you reckon
Will you come or will you stay?
Personally, I'm ready to do things in a new way
A second chance
To laugh, be free, to dance
Embrace a new way of being with open arms
So what you saying, will you stay or will you come?
Let's walk together towards the sun
Leave yesterday in the past
Because what's done, is done
Let's embrace this fresh opportunity like 2021 has only just begun.

The Rising After the Night Before

Cacao stains underneath your coffee cup

The faint smell of incense still lingers in the air

The sting of Sananga now a distant memory

As is the beat of the drum

Awakened ancestral memory now coursing through your veins

The present you merging with the former you

Some parts purged, never to be seen again

As the healing release sets you free from the shackles of who you thought you should be

And then comes integration

Sit with your thoughts and allow them to flow

Put pen to paper, meet the new you up close

Zoom in

Pan out

Stare into the reflection in the mirror

Look deep into your eyes

Hold that position for as long as you can

Then ask yourself in that moment

"who am I?"

The Hospital

In that hospital I saw life come, I heard life go
I met an ex-convict outside the CT scan room
He told me he couldn't leave the country
I told him my views on life
We both sat in that narrow corridor
Moments of silence peppered in between our exchange
I glanced at the bright yellow poster warning of the dangers behind that door
Three attempts it took them to get me to lay down in that room
One of the perks was getting wheeled around the secret passageways of the building
So quiet
A total juxtaposition against the lights, sounds and smells of the adjacent walkways
I assisted a tired trainee who became bewildered by the mother to be groaning in agony
Vomiting violently
That reaction induced by being administered something that doesn't come naturally
Moments later I watched her being whisked away
No doubt on her return she would never be the same
And I waited my turn
The skies became my solace
That was another good thing about being trapped in there
The bed beside the window
It was so expansive
I watched night turn to day and day turn to night
Those moment
The minutes
The hours
The days
Much of it spent alone
Gifted me
perspective

Growth

This period has seen me addicted to learning

More about me, about the world

In learning more about me

In turn, I learn more about you too

Naturally I've outgrown certain circumstances, people and places

But I guess new landscapes is what comes naturally when you seek to dig beneath the soil of that which you've always known

The fontanelle is the fount of all knowledge.

Time

When we stay home

we can't avoid that annoying pile of washing

the seemingly never ending dishes

the fingerprints

the post

with nowhere to be and nobody to see

it forces us to look in the mirror and see ourselves

without the veil of having to be here, there and everywhere

staying homes shines a light on the shadows we like to sweep under the rug

we could "flag it" or "mark as read" and add it to the "to do" list that might never get done

but really, with nothing else much to do and time on our side, the time is now

So what are we waiting for?

The Removal of the Veil – The Great Awakening

I took my vows as you took yours
You lifted the veil
A contract was sealed
The kiss of life
But then things changed
We saw the truth and from that moment on, nothing was the same

Soul Recognition

I swear I've seen your face before

Could you have been a childhood acquaintance or a lover from once upon a time

Or perhaps we were arch enemies on a battlefield

Maybe it wasn't your face I saw, perhaps it was your soul

So familiar to me

Tell me, do you remember me too?

Or could this be all but a dream

Growing Pains

It is an ache

A process taking place that feels unfamiliar

Inevitable, but not yet able to be articulated

Confusion and frustration

It is seen but not heard

Dying to one's former self

It is self- mastery

Independence

Shedding of the skin

A shift

Time to leave the chrysalis, to spread your wings and fly.

Endurance

This really is a marathon of extreme endurance
It's like the end is in sight
But not in clear focus

As I grow

As I grow and transcend limitations
I sow seeds and empower those around me

Permission to Rest

Rest now my darling
Nothing more, nothing less
Simply,
allow
yourself
...to rest.

Sweet Dreams Queen

Sweet dreams queen
Rest well
Your purpose is lofty and your intentions pure
I am in awe
I've observed the silent challenges you endure
Lay down,
Remove your majestic crown
take this moment as your permission to rest
A divine interlude before your next quest
Sweet dreams queen
I know you carry the weight of change on your shoulders
Tomorrow is a new day and you'll make your mark before it is over
So, lay down my queen,
I bid you good night, God bless and sweet dreams

Reflections on rest

Why is it that we accept a mere 14 out of 365 days to rest, do we not deserve more?

Grief and Gratitude

The pain eased (dissipated)
the moment I transmuted grief
into gratitude

Shattered

Is when the internalisation of the grief becomes so unbearable that you implode from within, allowing your heart to be broken, open, after a period of darkness the light comes flooding in, broken, open…shattered

CHAPTER 7
INNER CHILD

The most important relationship I will ever have, is with myself.

Born to be seen and heard

The ache in my throat disappeared, the moment I set free all the words left unspoken

Through the Eyes of a Child

Do you remember what it felt like to look up at the infinite black sky in awe of all the stars,

to laugh and jump and stomp and scream, regardless of where you are

when at the first sight of rain, you didn't complain, but rejoiced at the thought of wet muddy games!

You'd tilt your head back and open your mouth hoping to catch a falling drop if you could.

What was it made of, was it bad to drink? You didn't waste time trying to overthink.

All you knew is that it was water and air and if there was anything else in there, you just didn't care!

Back then alarms and bells meant freedom and playtime adventures, not hauling yourself out of bed to go work with miserable strangers

when a blanket and chairs were more than furnishings, but a portal to other places - a tent, a tepee in a forest with rainbows or a desert with dunes your peaceful oasis

When risks were opportunities to take those crazy forbidden leaps!

When cardboard boxes were not viewed as clutter, but places to hide and go seek.

When fences and walls, real or imagined, were not boundaries to new promised lands,

when you climbed and scaled with all of your might, despite grazing your knees and hands.

Although you may get weary, vision blurred with tears of life

Sometimes, take it back to when you saw the world around you, through the eyes, of a child.

Safe Place

I will keep you safe and cherish you for the rest of my days

I carry your innocent spirit like a delicate porcelain chalice overflowing with love

I will wipe your tears and hold your secrets safe in a trinket of everlasting nurture

You, my darling, have my everlasting promise that I will never desert you

A letter from the Tooth Fairy

many times

when something goes

it is often making way

for something even more beautiful

Rainbows and Roses

You see that's the beautiful thing about rainbows and roses

They may not appear every day

And they may not flourish in every season

But when they do

Isn't it magical?

No Title

The black girl
The black woman
The only child for quite some time
The eldest child
The good girl
The mother
The wife
The dutiful daughter
The employee
The strong one
The descendent of those who has their true power supressed in order to contort to fit in spaces that could never really be considered home
The societal conditioning
Layers upon layers stored within the emotional field causing what I can only describe as energetic constipation that I wasn't aware that was there until that moment.
You see, many of us are walking around with unseen emotional blockages in the gut, head and heart
To give it an image, it's like a sacred sacral fire burning beneath the surface, ready to blaze when seen and stoked
Truth is, I'm not sure when I 've been asked to be held- if ever?
I mean I know I have been, but usually it's in the moment of crisis
And sometimes people just haven't has the capacity when I needed and sometimes, I just haven't allowed it to happen.
I thank you my spirit, ancestors and you beautiful humans for holding me so lovingly
Thank you for being my anchor, for your hugs, for your heart, for your smile, for your authority, for your humility, for your courage, for your truth, for your laughter, for your willingness, for your persistence.
Thank you for making me feel safe enough to peel back the layers of lifetimes and stand in my true essence.
Thank you for being the mirror and the medicine
What a divinely timed release
Eye love you

Choose You

She kept choosing them

Choosing that

Next time

One day

When that…

After this…

Till one day she said “eff it”

I’m choosing myself

Growing Older with Grace

As we age with grace

the deep creases within our skin resemble that of the aged bark of a tree

each line representing a story of a time gone by

with every additional metre of height

comes a stronger grounding of wisdom

Destiny determines the destination, but free will determines the route.

CHAPTER 8
HEALING

You are your greatest healer, the answers are held within.

Through the Looking Glass

Through mirrors of my own deepest wounds
I saw reflections of abandonment
By others
Of self
Secrets and lies
Surface wounds
Soul deep
Scars partially healed
Only to have the plaster ripped off
More than once
Sometimes by my own doing
They say the lessons will repeat themselves until the student has finally learned
Glad to say I graduated a few classes
Perhaps still repeating some
Such is life
Seasons and cycles
The wheel keeps turning
Sometimes life will leave your head spinning
Joyful like the waltzer ride
Its heady and full of pleasure
And then it stops
And you realise its time to get off
Shaky legs
Sweaty palms
Is the earth beneath your feet spinning?
Or is that a misconception?
Everything comes down to perception

I lost items of sentimental value
I wanted to scream for the ache it caused
A void that cannot be replaced
Only an earring to some
But everything to me
I said I needed to master non-attachment
And so, the cosmos handed it to me on a plate
One that I watched as it fell
Shattered
Accept it
Let it go
Go with the flow
Sometimes that's easier said than done
When it's all said and done
But I'll keep growing
The world will keep turning
Our paths intertwine
Your lessons become mine
Until the wounds are healed
The scars begin to fade
And the reflection of that life lesson dissolves
And is gradually replaced

It Wasn't Your Fault

"It wasn't your fault" these words came to me in a meditation some time ago and have stuck with me ever since.

So many wounded people are walking through life perpetuating behaviours that they were taught by other wounded people. So much of what is wrong within the collective stems from pain, confusion, broken hearts and stolen dreams.

If we were to strip it all back, we would realise we've veered so far from nature, that it's inevitable that we would suffer and be the cause of pain.

So much is being undone at this time to strip back to our true nature, to open our hearts to what our soul knows to be true. Some souls simply got lost along the way. So whilst I believe in accountability, I also recognise that in many ways, to a large degree, it wasn't our fault.

However, once you become consciously aware of a different way, the onus is then on you to chose different and every single day you rise again, God has gifted you that opportunity to make that choice.

With that awareness does come difficulties, but the awareness is the calling and once you take that call, you will be the guiding light for generations down to the line that you will never even meet.

All of this, all of it, is the mirror for the journey to see deeper back into yourself…

Intimacy

Intimacy is not easy

Intimacy calls for the cracks to be seen, the buries parts to be unearthed, for the hidden truths to be revealed, to be held, to be nurtured, for forgiveness and compassion.

Sometimes it requires space whilst you gather an innerstanding.

It's triggering

Sometimes it is tears and frustration, it rips off the scabs to wounds that we thought we had transcended .

Ultimately, it is the deepest kind of love, because it's real..

Some said 2020 was a write off, I say it's the plot twist we never knew we needed.

2020 Healing

What is happening right now is a huge purge that I believe is beyond just the physical.
With all that is going on in the world it can feel exhausting, but at the same time, if the energy is used correctly, we will be able to look at this time as liberating
What we are witnessing right now is a release of generations of emotions.

Many of us have been entrenched in that saying “keep calm and carry on”
Many of us have also benefitted at the detriment of others and carry guilt
A lot of us have been denied apologies which others have been given freely and fell betrayed.

All of that subconscious unresolved baggage weighing down the hearts and minds of many.
This release is a huge cry, a permission to exhale.
Watching and feeling this release play out as a collective, is deep, all of our stories and the roles we have played, unique but enmeshed.

Someone once said to me that every family has its secrets, what is happening on the planet right now feels like a huge exposure of a secret that was always hidden in plain sight.

It’s complex, the feelings are many and they come in waves, like stages of labour, or that guttural grief when you feel a bereavement or the first time you experience heartbreak, it isn’t pretty, but the release and all that comes with it is necessary.

And in this public spectacle of release, don’t underestimate the immensity of navigating the rollercoaster of your emotions in private. The grief, frustration, connection, anger, hope, sadness, unity, resentment, liberation, emancipation, happiness, joy and love.

How it looks and feels cannot be linear.

We have to remember we are navigating a global pandemic and all that comes with that, agendas and narratives that may not align with out highest good. As well as realisation of outdated systemic constructs which need to be broken down and rebuilt.

Whatever we label this time as, as exhausting as it has been at time, I am thankful and holding space for my own and the collective release right now because it is in and after the release, that births the way for true healing..

Cutting chords will allow you to float to the highest realms awaiting you.

Solitude

There is a difference between loneliness and solitude.

Solitude is like a spring clean for the soul, it helps you to attune or re-tune to your own frequency.

Pleasure and Purpose

you see
the pleasure is integral to the purpose
If there is no pleasure in the purpose
the purpose becomes a chore

The End

and then it ended
the tears
the tragedy
the drama
the joy
the years
the fears
the trust
the love
the lust
over
in the beat of two broken hearts

Grief

In indigenous tribes' grief is expressed through wailing, screaming and rituals that span days

Maybe we could learn from them

Let us not to mute our pain to protect the fragility of others.

Nine

I was nine when they told me

In that moment my little mind tried to process the gigantic information that I did not bear the weight of before then

In that moment my heart broke

I tried to make sense of it all

What was real

What was imagined

Who was I

Why

And suddenly those hushed conversations

Those veiled remarks

Made sense

They asked me if I was okay and no sooner could they complete their sentences, I responded in a way that would never lead them to believe I was anything but that

But truthfully

Underneath the layer of a smile

Deep down

From there

I carried shame and guilt and grief

It shattered my sense of trust

One day I ran up to that one friend in the playground and I told her this secret of mine

Perhaps wanting someone else to share the weight of what I now knew

Perhaps wanting to see her reaction

On reflection, maybe that was the first test of me using my voice

Of healing myself

In some way the start of freeing myself

It was years until I uttered that secret again

But yes, when you look back on your life you will realise that there were many catalysts that sparked your healing journey

Mine, was nine.

Full Moon In Cancer – She's Deep

Curving around your cosmos, something like a celestial orbit

Tell me

Are you afraid of heights?

Because I wanna take you to the stars and further afar

Will you swim beyond the shallow end?

Or are you afraid to drown?

Would you run with wolves and play with lions and tigers if I asked you to?

Can you hold it down?

Be an anchor when the seas get rough

Or a compass if we need a change of direction?

Listen I know it's a lot of questions

But

Can you sit in silence when it's needed, take a moment for quiet reflection?

Will you teach me things I'm yet to learn, be patient and understanding?

Pick me up if ever I should fall

Sit me down when I need grounding

Because I would do that all for you

So let's make a wish and let it come true

Whilst heavenly lucid astral dreaming

Under the light of a beautiful bright full moon

Everything that has happened to date, has prepared you for exactly where you are now.

One man's poison, is another man's pleasure

You drink alcohol to shift your state of mind

I drink plants to shift my state of being

The spirits you evoke as you swallow that liquid so strong it burns your throat

What dimension are they from?

When I swallow the cacao, elixir of the sun

it blasts open my heart, a portal to the infinite one

Don't get me wrong, this isn't to judge or diminish what you do

I used to drink those spirits once upon a time too

You see, one man's poison, is another man's pleasure

Light melts into darkness

And souls become tethered

Whatever you take

Do so with intention

And what I will say is this

Unlike manufactured liquor, the plants are a blessing

They will alter your state of matter and transport you to higher heights

Both have the power to lead you to your truth

One with an intermediary

The other, the only translator is you

Imagine

Imagine being told your whole life that you were bottom of the pile
Last in the line
The ladder, no rungs for you to climb
Most likely to die
That your hair was wrong
Your skin less desirable
Your voice too loud
Aggressive
Angry
Sexualised by most
Demonised by many

But then

Imagine this

Imagine waking up from that slumber
To realise that the black womban is to be revered
That she ruled over kingdoms and led the greatest of quests
That she gave birth to nations
And that within her hips hold the DNA to most beings
That her hair is so powerful it's like a vortex of energy
That the fact that it defies gravity is to be admired
Not vilified
That the fertile lands from whence she came are so abundant

They hold wealth, true wealth, that would outlive generations for millennia

Diamonds

Gold

Bauxite

Uranium

Water

Iron

Sugarcane

Oil

Imagine discovering much of that which we enjoy today was created by a black man, who was birthed by a black man

Imagine!

Imagine that

Grieving

I know I stopped grieving when I could listen again to songs that remind me of you

Realisation reflections

It can be both daunting and liberating the moment you realise that only you have the answers to all the questions you hold within

Living Prayer

Let me be a living prayer of self love and devotion

And if it so be

Let that depth of love I find within me

Lead me all the way home, back to you.

Beauty In a Blade of Grass

They who find beauty in a blade of grass, will find beauty in all living things

Audacious Humans

What

You really thought you could go on and on and on

Polluting my skies

Littering my seas

And I would let you carry on without bringing you to your knees?

I sent you plenty warnings

Weathered storm after storm after storm

But still you kept on littering

Ignoring the cries from my heart

I hope you take this period of reflection as a gift from me to you

And when all of this is over, you'll change the things you do

Extinctions and changes are written in scripture – yes the ones you said you read on Sundays

So why did you miss my messages from Monday through to Saturday

The song goes that joy and pain is like sunshine and rain

When you've learned your lessons darling

Ill let you out again

With love

Always in all ways

Your mother, Nature

Fear

Feel it she said, truly feel it all.

Often times we want to push it away, overcome it even, but this time, allow yourself to feel it. What does it feel like, how does it taste.

What does it look like?

And so I pondered on that perspective and surrendered to the feeling, and in that moment the truth appeared.

How does it feel I replied …"it feels dark and lonely".

A Portal of Love

may you take solace in this space

rest your head against my beating heart

and lean deep into the knowing

that all of you is welcome here

Life is fleeting but to be enjoyed. You deserve better, the best. By being better to you, you make decisions that align with your divine purpose. You are so worthy and so loved. Not only will you be okay, but you will thrive, I promise!

Self Love

Sometimes we can spend far too long searching for love and approval inside a darkened cave when really all we need to do is turn around and step up into our own internal light of self-love.

It's okay to sit in the pain, don't bypass it, but know that soon, it will pass!

Realisation

The most ground-breaking, soul shaking moment for me came
when I realised it was not you, him or her that broke my heart
it was me-
it was me who broke my own heart by denying myself what I
knew I always needed to sustain its most beautiful rhythm

Kintsugi or "golden joinery" or golden repair, is the Japanese art of repairing broken pottery by mending the areas of breakage with powdered gold, silver, or platinum.

The alchemy of life and new moon energy. Observing the pots in my garden, shattered by the cold temperatures. The global crumbling of old systems and structures and the dulcet tones of Jhene Aiko playing thru my speakers inspired this one…

Kintsugi

As she sat surrounded by the shards of her heart

She decided to pick up each tiny fragment

One by one

And whilst it took her quite some time

What she was able to put back together was far more beautiful than she could ever have imagined.

Strength and Struggle

Strength doesn't have to be synonymous with struggle

Pondering on strength and struggle I realised a few things

That strength can also be synonymous with softening and vulnerability

That I could be strong without struggling

That sometimes we create our own struggles, making situations more complex than necessary

That it's okay to admit when we are struggling

That strength is sometimes silent

That a holistic approach and awareness of mind, body and soul alignment, is the foundation of the best kinds of strength

Yes… on reflection, you can be both strong and struggle simultaneously and I have no doubt that in this season with 2020 hindsight all of us have shown and felt both.

Notes on Forgiveness

I forgive you for only being able to meet me as far as you could meet yourself, will you forgive me for the same?

I understand that your actions towards me were merely a reflection of your inner realm

I also understand that it was the unhealed parts of you and I that sometimes triggered the worst

As much as it has hurt, and whist I will always seek to honour my pain by seeing where it lays and soothing it how I can, I too, am sorry for any pain that I may have caused you

In it all I thank you for the part you have played in teaching me exactly what it was I needed to learn more about myself.

Seeing Through the Lens of Love

Help me to see only through the lens of love and purity

for I know that everything I see outside of me,

is simply a reflection of that which resides inside of me

Unpicking The Tapestry of History

I am unpicking the tapestry of the lies that were woven by his-story so I can get to the heart of the true story

What Makes a Healer?

You are a healer I am a healer. Many people you meet or circumstances you have on a day-to-day basis, provide the opportunity to provoke your healing and give you insights that can literally change the course of your life. Some people have natural healing auras and energy. Some go to schools to learn how to heal using specific modalities. I have studied both the spiritual and physical aspects of healing, but really it is my heart, energy and a natural affinity to love and want the best for myself and others.

I have always been a space holder for others in various ways, before I was even consciously aware of what it is that I was doing. Intuition and empathy comes naturally because it is interwoven in the fabric of my DNA. It also comes from things I have overcome, lessons learned and experienced in this lifetime and maybe times prior.

One of the greatest things I have learned, is that in order for me to hold space for you, I have to ensure I hold space for myself. I am not perfect, but I am self aware and love to get to the root cause of why things happen the way they do.

Transcending painful stories and recreating the experience you desire is powerful work, not only for you but for everyone who ever comes into contact with you and also for your bloodline.

This could be as simple but profound, as being the first in your entire family to stop smoking, or being the first to embark on healing, to being the first to create intergenerational wealth.

Whether you describe yourself as a healer or not, it is imperative that you invest in and take care as best you can of your physical, mental and spiritual health. It is also important that what you do as a space holder is with discernment and the purest intention for the highest good of all.

To me, a good healer is someone who will hold you with love but also holds a mirror for you to see yourself and be your own healer. This can sometimes be triggering but that is a sign that you are bringing to the surface what you have tried to hide from yourself. A true healer will also learn from you and is honoured to be a guide. They will signpost you to other services that will help you on your way and will not encourage you to be co-dependent on them forever. They want to see you flourish and only return when and if you truly need to.

Into Me See ~ Intimacy

Intimacy is not easy, intimacy calls for the cracks to be seen, the buried parts to be unearthed, for the hidden truths to be revealed, to be held, to be nurtured.

For forgiveness and compassion, sometimes space whilst you gather an understanding.

It's triggering, it's sometimes tears and frustration, it rips off the scabs to wounds we thought were healed.

Sometimes it's a repeat of cycles we thought we had transcended.

Ultimately, it's the deepest kind of love, because it's real.

Never Alone

When I'm at one with myself I know I'm never alone
Divine assignment
Introspection
For I am my first home
Don't get me wrong, sometimes it's dark
But the light always returns
When my mind body and soul are in alignment
It sets a spark to a flame that will forever burn

Never alone, never alone, you are never alone
I know your thoughts sometimes get overwhelming when you get in that zone
Turn down the volume on the chatter and tune into your soul
Calm your breathing
Hold your heart
And feel your life rhythm flow

When times get lonely you can call me
You are never alone
Whether it's for a chat or a laugh or a bit of a moan

I look at you and see your smile on the surface but underneath all of that I can see your soul is hurting.

Come,
let me envelope you with my love, embrace you with my arms
I will be your solace
We don't need words, be still, be silent,
Find peace,
calm.

You see you never know what someone may be going through - what happens behind that door
They'll tell you a part of the story but just know there's always more

Be kind, show compassion, I see you, you see me
that is true intimacy
for love is the highest frequency

This life is bittersweet, it has its ebbs and its flows, take the highs with the lows, grieve, breath, release, know when to let it go

Hold your head up to the sky and look into the stars
You'll See Infinite reasons to remember that you are perfect just as you are
Only look back into the chasm to see how far you have come
and if ever the loneliness returns

Call on God, your source, your guides and be reminded you are never alone.

In this new age, we are calling in a deeper level of intimacy, where we are more willing to accept ourselves and others- all of them, no façade, no mask – and that does not mean you tolerate that which isn't healthy for you, but it means you have a level of empathy in your relationships which is deeply healing, not easy, but healing.

Call upon relationships that allow you to bring all of you, where you are made to feel that every part of you, is welcome here.

The Elixir

A potent potion of magical mystery, one sip is never enough

More and more is never too much

Like a hug in a mug

The window to your soul

Enthralled with it all

The perfect tincture, go ahead, fill your cup

Heart Led Life

And so I guess when life shows you more than once that tomorrow is not promised, you stop putting off until tomorrow, what the heart desires today

Night vision - Afraid of the dark

I wonder if it is in our nature to be afraid of the dark

When the Amazonian tribesmen hunt, it is in the darkness that their vision becomes clearer

Plant medicine sharpening their perception

Perhaps it is in the dark where we find our truth

Senses heightened, no distraction

Laser focus

Not foresight, nor hindsight but a powerful spiritual insight

Golden Soul

If you knew the currency of your soul, you wouldn't be so quick to sell it

Yew

I humbly bow before you now

At 11:11

I bask in your majesty

I thank you for your wisdom

To think when you were planted as a seed all those years ago you knew not what your future would bear

I wonder of the lifetimes you have seen

The storms you have weathered

The shelter you have provided

Yew

Beautiful beautiful yew

I want you to know that as you stand there and many may pass you by

I see you

I thank you

Yew

The love of A Mother

It is only when you are gone that I can put down my shield
Let down my guard
The protector rests her armour
Sinks into her pillow
Closes her eyes
Pours out her heart
And allows the tears to flow
And flow they do
Freely
A deep release
These tears, they carry love, they carry heartbreak, they carry grief
They also carry joy, love and cleansing healing
Release
Release
relief

Make me a Channel

Use me, I am yours
An open empty vessel
Pluck my strings softly
Make a beautiful melody and turn it into a symphony

Reflection

When you look in the mirror there may be lots of parts you love or there may be parts that you don't
Only you will know
But that's sort of like our lives and everyone in it
Everyone
Every thing
Is the mirror
And even though it may appear on the outer
All of it
Is the reflection of what is on the inner

Know Thy Self

The only ones who benefit from you not knowing who you are, are the ones who know exactly who you are.

Intuition

And how willing are you to trust the innate knowings, even when they come ahead of time and seem bizarre?

With all my heart is how much

And she said “why”

And I replied “because the writing is on the wall”

So she said “but how do you know”

And that is when I said “I don’t know how I know, I just know, the writing holds the codes, sort of like braille to a blind person. It’s often when we close our eyes that we see the most

In the light and in the dark, my spirit is my torch and my soul is my guide

A spire sits atop cathedral

It is the conductor of energy

So too is your crown

Do you trust your inner spire, your inner tutor, your intuition?

I surely trust mine.

Cutting Chords

I release you

the time we shared

the parts that felt good

and the parts that were difficult

I release you

I release me

goodbye

Songs That Remind Me of You

It was when I could listen to those song that remind me of you without feeling sad, that I knew I was no longer grieving

Empathy

If you can come through the fire with
your heart intact, the empathy you
gain will be a gift to the universe

Shine

I hear you have talents and dreams
that you diminish for fear of making
some feel inadequate in your light.
Don't do that, don't you know that
your light will act as a beacon for
those behind you, if you only you
allow it shine.

Adventures

The magic will not be found on a screen and the best bits will not usually be captured on camera, but trust me, it exists

It's in the stars in the sky, the unseen energies as they pass you by, the butterflies, the faces in the sky, the telepathic communication and the knowing look in the horse's eye

The dragonflies that hover to you by the rivers and streams, the swans, the herons, the majestic trees

Its when you take off that mask and allow yourself to breath, to be, its away from the concrete jungle and where there are lush lands that go so much further than your eyes can see

Its beyond the limitations we place on ourselves, its when we listen within and follow the signs, guided by the heart's desires and God's design

There is always magic to be made and magic to be seen

The moment that you start to believe in it, trust me, you'll see.

Finding Yourself

you aren't finding yourself,
yourself was always there
beneath the layers
beneath the labels
beneath the conditioning
beneath the trauma
there you were
always

Sowing Seeds

Spread your light and sow seeds that will blossom beyond your physical existence

I Had To Leave

I had to leave you, in order that I could find myself

Beyond the Horizon

Eye wanna go as far as the eyes can sea and then some.

Learning to Respond versus react

When they tell you they admire your strength, don't take that as an invitation to react, ready for battles that aren't yours to fight. One day you will know, the biggest bout you can win, is the one of responding versus reacting- the latter being the only opposition you need to conquer.

Detox

When density screams at me

I realise I am blocking my own energy

I want God source to flow through me freely

So, I must clear my vessel intermittently

And when I do, it clears my channels so beautifully

Attracting pure abundance!

And releasing scarcity

Family

Family is comfort

Family is kinship

Family is complex

Family is friendship

Family will challenge you

The landscape may change

It is ever evolving

But the love will always remain

Reflection or deflection?

What is it about you, that I see in me?

Is it our differences that trigger me, or could it be our similarities?

The woman on the train

I don't know you

And you don't know me

But I want you to know I see you

Do you see me?

Conversations With You Via God

You know that God speaks to you in a number of ways right?

Be it that conversation with an aunt

Those words from a stranger

The stars dotted amongst a clear night sky

The oceans and rivers as their waves break the shore

A line in a book that catches your eye

Through the changes in your body

The frequency of your heart

God is always speaking to us

God is *always* speaking through us

All we have to do is be silent, drawn near and receive…

The journey

You see that's the thing …

Perhaps you aren't meant to know the destination.

Maybe plotting every single step of the route isn't the way, perhaps.

Perhaps, you are meant to trust in a higher guidance

Knowing that there is a journey that you are meant to take which God Source and your angels will help you navigate

Perhaps toss that map away

And give caution to the wind

Don't force and fight

Fly and flow

Like the buds of the beautiful Pussy Willow.

Fate

Your path was paved in gold

Your destiny inscribed on ancient scrolls

Long before you were even a twinkle in your father's eye or implanted in your mother's womb

Your existence is a series of fated moments that has led you to this here moment...can you imagine if your life was made into a movie or a novel? Your life is poetry in motion and every chapter has its place.

Lightwork

Being a "light worker" means focussing on raising the vibes but not playing dumb to the dark- both exist and you have to shine the light on both. When you use a torch, yes it illuminates the path, but it also highlights the pitfalls

Manifestation

When you boldly admit that you want that thing you were afraid to admit you wanted,

The universe will ultimately deliver unto you that very thing.

Quantumn Physical

Let's get quantum physical explore the inner workings of our inner souls

Inner sun

Right down to the nitty gritty

Every single itty bitty part of me

Zoom right in

Use your biggest lense

Telescopes and horoscopes

See into me

Maybe do some telepathy

The affinity between you and me goes on into infinity

And beyond

Buzz has nothing on us

The way our cells dance when we become one

That magical vibration

Charging up under the sun

One minute we're talking nonsense

The next, protons and photons

You turn me on

You stimulate my vegus nerve

Creating electricity

Synergy

Harmony

Unity

Entertwined ehterically

In a place that reaches far beyond what they eyes can see

When our eyes are closed it's through the first eye that we conceive

Wild imagination
No limitations
Reaching for the sun moon and stars without hesitation
For thoughts become things sending magnetic waves
As our synapses pave the way
The big bang or divine intervention
Immaculate conception

Still

Still loving the birds

Sill listening out for the bees

Still hugging the odd one or two trees

Still running through fields of green

Still watching the brook water glean

Still gazing in awe up at the clouds

Still watching the sun as she goes down

Still thanking God as I kneel to pray

Still grateful for each new day

STILL

Still me, still free.

Self love

It’s not that I no longer love you,

It’s that I no longer love you to the
detriment of loving me

Frequency is a feeling. Just like you can fine tune a radio to your desired station, you can also attune your own frequency by doing things you love. You will know if something is your authentic frequency by how it makes you feel. Your body ad intuition always gives clues, it's just that sometimes we choose not to listen in.

When you don't stay true to your own frequency you'll get static feedback, like when the aerial on the old style radios can't quite pick up the station.

As you change your frequency you may find that the old stations i.e., spaces, people and things that used to feel good, no longer will, and that's okay. Just as you have a radio that has hundreds of stations you can choose from and know exist, or co-exist. You can relax in the knowing that you can coexist with those on different frequencies to a degree, but always remain true to you by tuning into what feels right.

Energy Speaks Louder Than Words

Some go by the belief that your reputation precedes you,
I go by the belief that your energy precedes you.

Rich

My energy is my currency

Mother was tired

Mother was tired and needed a rest
Her body showed signs, yet we kept putting her to the test
Going and going, carrying it all
Bag by bag
Hitting the wall
Day by day
Load by load
Feeling as though she would implode

You didn't hear, so she made you feel

Kneel
Sit
Stop
Stand still

All so that she could take the time she really deserved and needed, to begin
To heal.

Self-Love

It's not that I no longer love you

It's that I no longer love you to the detriment of loving myself.

Finding Yourself

You aren't finding yourself you were always there, beneath the layers, beneath the labels, beneath the trauma…there you were, always.

Self Care

Self care is non- negotiable

Self care is sacred

The Whole Truth

In me honouring my truth I am not only honouring myself, I am honouring you too.

Your Truth

They tell you to speak your truth but
when you do, they go silent.

My higher self is my best friend

I am putting down fear for it is an illusion. I am calling in protection and peace, inner wisdom

I will listen to and act upon my inner voice. I will follow her, trusting that she is leading me to my ascension, she loves me so much and is holding me, always.

Don't try to supress me from greeting the divine within me, just because you're not yet ready to acknowledge the divine within yourself.

Goddess

Goddess of motherhood, fertility and healing

Daughter of the sky Goddess and Earth God. Magician, trickster, protected by seven scorpions

The solar disc is the symbol of my name

I am the mistress of magic

Goddess of life and death

I am rebirth

With wings as long as kites

Red jasper and an ankh by my side

I produce life from my own source energy

Unselfish lover of all

I am the original divine mother

My wings span far and wide and will wrap you in love for all eternity

Ebbs and Flows

A wave never stays the same my love

There is beauty in the ebbs and the flows

The highs and the lows

Without navigating the troughs of the mountain tops, how could you ascent to the height of the peaks

A wave never stays the same my love

It ebbs and it flows

Take the highs and the lows

Trust the tide will take you where you need to go

So lean in

Don't fight

Release

Surrender

And breath

I am a multifaceted multidimensional divine creation of flowing energy that will be honoured as it flows and however it flows, I will let it flow.

Tantric

You say you wanna explore the cosmos of my mind
Well first you need to enter through my heart
Maybe then I'll let you explore the landscape of my soul
From there, the body will follow, naturally ...

Intuition

I can read you like a book
Yet I don't need your words
Intuition tells me all I need to know
I tune in as your story unfolds
Turning the pages with intrigue
Chapter after chapter
Lifetimes weave imagery
As I unfurl your divine tapestry
I'm transported into the heart of your inner world
Our souls, merged
Delighted by the insights
Given to me by my higher heart, higher mind, third eye.

Intuition part 2

Shhhh, don't speak

I'm in tuition with my inner tutor
M'eye teacher
My higher self
My angel guides
I don't need words
She already knows...

Tiger stripes – Feline Fine

Come a little closer

Study every single nook of my savanna

“What are those you ask?”

“They” I reply “are my tiger stripes…go ahead and read between the lines”

Lioness

Shhh not too loud

Ooooh that's a bit tight

They might get the wrong idea

Bit too much passion

Supress your pain

Who do you think you are?

Who does she think she is!

What will the neighbours say?

...all that restriction

All that contortion

All that suppression

Held in the sacral chakra

Blocking your heart

Dimming your light

Taming your fire

But it stops here

In this lifetime

Rise

They didn't bank on us awakening to our divine essence

But my darling,

It

Is

Time

Inside Out

Don't talk

Just listen

Could it be that your higher self is in fact your future self?

How willing are you trust that perspective

To free fall into the void knowing that you will be caught, held...

Are you brave enough to trust the signs?

To witness and better yet, acknowledge rather dismiss them as mere coincidences?

Losing track of time as the timelines merge and converge

getting lost in time is divine

weaving in and out of dimensions

feeling tipsy because the sand timer has been turned upon its head and every single particle is now rearranging itself to fall in line

it's a powerful time

community with those in energetic alignment is wonderful and in fact, a necessity

so to, is asserting your energetic sovereignty

those lions at your gate serve as a guard of discernment for who comes in and out of your domain

but remember the lion is courageously led by the heart, so whilst you protect the boundary, along with your intentions, allow room for play and connection

because the lion is not lone for too long, their power lays in the strength of their pride.

00:32

On reflection

perhaps like a river

people who are not in alignment with me are flowing out of my frequency

and perhaps that is not a loss, but a gift

Grand Risings

As I bend and slide

Take some deep and mindful breaths and feel it rise

I awaken a vortex of energy

Some refer to it as sahaja, jnana or kriya

Others, Kundalini

Electric Energy

Cycles

Determined not to get caught in a monthly cycle that sees me back at square one

determined to progress

lay the habits, people, places and spaces that no longer serve me to rest

to take accountability for where it's not him, her or them – but me

Wash away any hidden pain

Start again

I'm ready

Full moon

Big tides

Take it all away so I can thrive

Fully

I don't want to repeat this loop again

They say doing the same thing over and over expecting different results is insane

So I take it to the sea

Release it to be free

Full moon

Big tides

Accepting and letting go of what no longer is for me

Full moon

Big tides

Let them deal with their karma and I'll handle mine

Fill my cup only with all that I need

Accepting and letting go of what is no longer for me

Ultimate surrender

Ultimate release

Wounded love

It was the unhealed parts of me that were attracted to the wounded parts of you

It was in my healing that my perspective changed

An altered point of view

My vision no longer skewed

Self-love renewed

And, in deeply loving me, I am also loving you

Loving me, loving you enough to let you go

To set me free

With gratitude, grace, honour

I'll go, respectfully

Snakes and Ladders

Healing and spiritual growth can be a bit like a game of snakes and ladders. One step forward, ten steps back

You'll climb the ladder and feel like you're on the fast track, only to come across a snake that may take you all the way back

But that's okay, keep rolling baby, keep rolling.

Spinning Plates

I am not one of the many plates you try to spin
You dropped me once and I broke into pieces
I put myself back together again
So, before you attempt to pick me back up
I suggest you leave me on the mantel piece
Pride of place
To admire from
a distance
Whist you keep on spinning them plates

Many times, hindsight provides 20/20 vision.

Dare to Dream

I could never trust you with my dreams,

Each time I shared them with you, you took the scroll upon which they were scribed and you ripped them to shreds

Time and time again I would run to you eagerly willing to share my latest divine insight

Only to be met with mockery and to be called a fraud

As I reclaim all parts of me and dare to openly dream my dreams

I realise now that you only tore down my hopes and reduced me to tears

Because my big and bright and beautiful dreams

Shone a mirror upon your deepest fears

Life Lessons

I have learned some of my most profound lessons at funerals

How a person has lived

Who they have loved

If they followed their dreams

The relationships that didn't work and years wasted on arguing and hate

If you were to know these were your last moments on earth, or the last moments of others in your life- what would you do differently?

Don't let pride stand in the way of sending that text, saying how you feel, or making that visit

When really, all everything comes down to, is love

Affliction

I know this may sound like a contradiction
but sometimes I wish I had an addiction to
numb these feelings of affliction
but my guides won't let me go there
so instead
I sit with it
to feel it is to heal it
or so they say
and feeling it, I am.

Blanc Page

There is something unnerving about a blank white page, the gift and the curse is that there is nothing there to work with, but maybe it is wonderful that there is nothing there to work with. Perhaps it's not such a curse after all. Perhaps the gift is that you finally get to be the author of your very own story.

Lessons

How many times would it take for me to hear the words “I didn’t ask you to” rolling so flippantly off of the edge of their tongues before they cut deep enough for me to realise that the love I kept pouring out, was the love that I needed to pour within

Vows

What If we were to tear
down these walls and
rebuild a lifetime

Reflections of Love Through a Shattered Mirror

When you develop an image of love through a mirror that was shattered the voice in your head rules when it's the song in your heart that truly matters

You have the understanding that love should be patient and kind, but how so when the reality is unstable, volatile

Pillars of strength made in broken homes, broken hearts, solid bones, skewed misconstrued, is this love or contradiction, fantasy, reality, comedy, fiction.

I bear the weight of rewriting history but with no blueprint to follow, some days it's just too much of a bitter pill to swallow, some days it's beyond me

Set the example, go left where they took a right, pick your battles, they said, when the urge is to fight

Just let it go, let love in, put down your guard

We don't want a love that is just a façade

Know better, do better, the kids are watching, but what can they do when mummy is crying

From the mouth of babes never a truer story told, they can see in your art that you exchange your soul for a pot of gold

I want to know you so much deeper, you bought me a house, so you must be a keeper

But I yearn not for the walls of that house on the lake, I yearn for an intimate bond that no one can break.

The world is watching, quick smile! Take a photo, but no sooner does the lens shut, it's a whole different picture …reflections of love through a shattered mirror.

Soul Food

Once you've sampled soul food, nothing else will ever taste the same.

Mother

A mother's love feels things without having to see things

Beyond the Umbilical Cord

Baby,

I want you to know that the love I hold in my heart for you is a bond that can never be severed

You are me and I am you

Our DNA is entwined in a dance that transcends time, space and matter

As night falls and the streets go quiet, it's just you and I, skin to skin

Heart to heart

In the dark I hold my ear to your mouth just to hear your breath

The beat of your heart is rhythm to my very own

As I watch you grow, taking steps of your own

I know

That one day you will no longer need my hand

But I'll always be there to guide you, lovingly, should you need me

Because, there is no greater love

CHAPTER 9
EMBODIMENT

In our healing journey we are often presented with choices, we recognise that our inner conflicts are often as a result of outer expectations. That recognition is mind blowing and can be the key to our freedom. Once we develop that awareness, we can then take steps to make the necessary changes in order to reach true self – acceptance.

We begin to realise what parts of our false identity no longer serve us and so, we begin a process of release. Dying to what and who you were conditioned to be and taking space as the full expression in the home of who you are.

.

Multifaceted

that's the beauty of humanhood
we are multifaceted beings
layers of light entwined with layers of darkness
a beautiful dichotomy ...and that's okay
just like a gorgeous gemstone
every
single
facet
is necessary.

Womban

Womban

Never underestimate your power

Those tiger stripes hold stories untold between each and every line

Made by God's design

A cosmic playlist

Sometimes it's calm like a classical harmony

Other times it's like an untuned orchestra without a conductor

Wild

Every curve a symphony

Bittersweet

Bearing fruits from the tree of life

Abundance

There is power between those thighs

You birth nations

Lifetime after lifetime

So womban

Never underestimate your power

And always remember that you are divine

Secrets and Synchronicities -Be Your Own Muse

She is bountiful

Naturally

Whatever you intentionally invest in her multiplies

Because *she* is the empress.

Her roots run deep as do her waters

Crowned by the celestial sun

Her energy is synonymous with divinity

There is no such thing as coincidence

When her scales are balanced its simply synchronicity

Upon synchronicity

Upon synchronicity

Magical

What's her secret? Whatever it is, you find it in a manual or a book up on your shelf

Covered by God

Her secret is source

So, if you want the answers

Go and look there

I am abundant and attracting all that aligns with my highest self!

I know the power of my presence, I know the power of my love, I know the power of my energy.

Her

She doesn't need pronouns to announce that which she is

Because who she is holds divine feminine energy, naturally

That inner G

Her embodiment is the announcement

Her heartbeat is the first sound you will hear

Because she is alive

Trumpets, sirens and the heavens proclaim her presence

Sometimes quiet and demure

Other times loud and ferocious

A blissful rainbow or a raging hurricane

Whatever it is, she's gonna honour her nature

And just as nature is duality

She will ensure that balance is restored by any means necessary

You came from her

And even when others may forget that

Still

She is and always will be

Womban

Who am I when I take away the labels and conditioning – who am I at the core of me?

Words can activate so much healing and power when used for good. Tell yourself and the universe that you are open to receive all that aligns with your highest good in this here moment and for your future self. Remember, your future self doesn't have to be some far- flung version in the distance, it is also the person who is simply the next moment away.

No Regrets

I'm not one for regrets

When I look back it's usually through a lens of reflection

Largely I'll reminisce on the sweet parts and take heed of the moments that leave a bitter taste

And when I've finished doing that

I face forward and keep going

One step at a time

Ever more conscious of which way I tread

I am a divine creator of my reality, it was written "ye are Gods" and I am a Goddess/ God attracting pure abundance.

Vibes

She's got that once in a lifetime kinda vibe.

What they think they know of you is none of your business. But what you know about yourself is key.

Art

I am a work of art

Poetry in motion

Black history in the making

A reflection of source

A creator

Enriched with abundance

Fierce protected

Divinely loved

Who were you before the world told you who you should be?

Spirit Animal Symphony

she was somewhat of a lone wolf
a soft kitten
and a fierce lioness
all rolled into one.

Keep it real, authenticity is an expression of love

I Dare You To Strip

No, not your clothes

I wanna see your soul

Will you share with me your wildest dreams?

Take me to the hidden secrets of your past

Let me get a taste of what's to come

Your future passions and pleasures

Removing the mask that they said you had to wear

Revealing the true you

In saying all that, I wonder if I dare to do the same?

Peeling back the layers

Willing to be completely free and not what and who society told us we should be

You show me yours and I'll show you mine

Go on, I dare you.

Lioness Rise

Shhh not too loud

Oooh that's a bit tight

They might get the wrong idea

Bit too much passion

Supress your pain

Who do you think you are?

Who does she think she is!

What will the neighbours say?

…all that restriction

All that contortion

All that suppression

Held in the sacral chakra

Dimming your light

Taming your fire

But it stops here

In this lifetime

RISE

They didn't bank on us awakening to our divine essence

But my darling

It

Is

Time

I have so much abundance here and now and am attracting more abundance in all areas of my life. Prosperity flows towards me with ease, just like the current of the infinite ocean.

Who Is She? (Reimagined)

A Goddess of art and mystery

She faces inward to find the answers she seeks, for she knows that her higher self is the greatest teacher she will meet

Her mind is akin to the cosmos

She holds pure sunshine within her heart

But don't take her kindness for weakness because there is ancient power behind her smile

Through every peak and pitfall, she'll be sure to rise and shine

Her crown everlasting and her cup ever full

Abundant as nature

Sensitive, yet strong and oh so bountiful

Supernatural

Once you tune in you soon realise that
being supernatural come supernatural

Libra

You fan the flames but also put out fires
Love deep but can easily dismiss those who disregard you
You fight for justice like your life depends on it but keep it calm observing what's what
See the beauty in everything
Love the aesthetically pleasing

The arts spark your creativity
Ever the optimist looking for the light in all
But when something isn't right, you heed the call
Could be in designer gear or market stall and still make it fashion
Make a decision at the drop of a hat
Scratch that part - who am I kidding!

You're a little bit dinner jazz and a little bit gangster rap
A little bit scotch bonnet and a little bit chamomile
You're the early night and the time of their life
A hot-headed lover and a perfect housewife

A little bit Ye with a dash of Mary Berry
An espresso martini and a miniature glass of sherry
Socks and sandals and boots that reach thigh high
To know a Libran is to love and be loved
So get you a Libra in your life

My energy is my signature.

Alchemists

We are majestic alchemists
We will take a bad situation and transform it into something beautiful
We have intuition that knows things without having to see things
We make space for vulnerability and in doing so, make way for healing.

No longer will we suffer in silence or be still on issues that matter.

If ever I faced a challenge in life, I'd call upon and embody the poise of the queens that came before me, head held high.

Not a stance for everyone, some may find the jewels of your crown too dazzling, but that's okay.

Reign on anyway.

CHAPTER 10
THE ELEMENTS

Some believe there are four key elements, others five or seven. I have had profound moments when I realised the importance of the elements, particularly earth, air, fire, water and ether.

Everything we see in nature is a reflection of the elements, earth, air, fire, water and ether. So too are we, every single element balanced perfectly to create the innate spark of life.

Fire was the catalyst of creation that brough you into existence, water your first home, air the breath of life and earth your home. Ether the cosmos outside and within.

We can also look at the elements in relation to consciousness and state of being.

The sun our plasma and solar battery, our energy giver and self-esteem. The light we hold within and exude to the world. Water, the depths, our emotions and intuition, our release- water leaves our body through orifices in a number of ways. Blood, sweat and tears being amongst the most obvious. Earth is the ground we stand upon, our roots, our ancestry and foundation. Air the bids eye view, a higher perspective and the breath of life, a cyclical representation of divine reciprocity, give and take. To me the ether is the infinity of a night sky dotted with stars that create universes both seen and unseen.

Fire

There was something about the flames that felt like home
Could it be the deep orange hues or the searing heat
Perhaps it reminded me of the village of another lifetime
Or purification processes with intent to start again
The way the flame danced almost had me in a trance
My feet tip toeing at the edge
The snap crack and pop of the sparks did not bring fear
In fact
They brought liberation
Release
There was something about the flames that lured me close
The cinders beneath my soles a warm embrace
Perhaps my energy was the fan to this flame
The flame of freedom that was calling my name
To be honest with you it could be that or a million other things
But there was something about the flames that felt like home

Palo Santo flames

Let the flames of the fire show you the way
Let the warm glow of the heat ignite passion within
Lighting your desires
And when the smoke dissipates, you will see clearly
Pure cleansed, free energy.

Air

You pick me up and take me away
Ascending me to higher heights
Showing me a new perspective
Floating on a natural high
Stars in my eyes
Take me away
I am yours

There is a reason why they say "I feel it in my waters". Forget how it looks, forget how it sounds, how does it feel?

Water

You were my first home
You held me safely for nine months, in darkness I knew that I was safe
Fluidity
Transparency
Safety, is what you mean to me
When I need cleansing, there you are,
you fill every single one of my cells with LIFE
Buoyancy
Vitality
Water
You heal me

Thank you Fire for the passion/creativity you ignite in me
Thank you air for ascending me to higher heights
Thank you water for cleansing me
Thank you Mother Father Earth for always supporting me

Infinite Water

If you want to know about the power of water
Look to mumma
That moment she lays on her new-born babe
The love floods like a river that has burst its banks
It cannot be measured nor contained
And that infinite water
Is expressed
As tears

Immersion

Just as a fish beneath the water
I love to be immersed
But I can be all the way in
Or I can be all the way out
Remember, remember, remember
I was your first home she waves
Sacred waters she says
I hold memories of a thousand lifetimes
And you, like a pearl waiting to be discovered
Was birthed upon my banks
I am the depths of the darkest ocean and the shallow sand upon the shore
I hold hidden treasures waiting to be unfurled
Be open to receive every last drop
But let it flow, don't force it
Sending ripples out into the abyss
I am the sweet release in your tears
Reciprocal and unconditional love is what we have
I pour into you fulfilling my cup with your divine love as you take what you need from mine
So my energy overflows
An infinite ebb and flow
Wash over me I am yours
Baptise me with your tides
As I submerse myself in complete surrender
My well never runs dry
It pours in abundance and is restored ten-fold
For you are the source
When you forget I will remind you with the crashing of the almighty waves.
Queen of cups her love is unbounded
In her element as she dances with the tide

Elemental Being

A queen knows how to harness the magic of the elements, for she knows that she is the physical manifestation of every single one of them.

Channelling

Let me tune out

Tap in

Download straight codes from source

Ignore the distractions

The only channel I need to stream is that

Of God

Eternal Flame

you may have thought that the turbulent storms of life would have put out her light

but all it did was fan her flame

so that she could burn brighter

spreading her divine eternal light wherever she would go.

Roots (*inspired by the felled willow tree*)

Foolishly you may tear me down

But you must have forgotten

My roots run deep into the unseen and my source and supply will never run dry

Pachamama

Your first home was water

Your life, like a walk through the fire

When you die your flesh is returned to the earth

Before you rise, rise, rise, to the eternal, into the ether

CHAPTER 11
LOVE

There are many different forms of love, the truest being unconditional love. Sometimes it is in the bittersweet situations that life presents that we are able to taste what that is.

In love…even when there has been shame, hurt, guilt, sadness, change and grief…at the start and heart of it all was love. Because when you came into being all you needed was love and all you knew in that first moment, was love.

At the beginning and end of it all, there is love. The alpha and omega.

Agape…

To live in love is the highest manner of existence.

May

I remember it like yesterday

I remember you being the quietest little baby on the ward

I remember feeling shy to speak to you aloud when it was just me and you

I remember lights out on the ward that first night

I remember the code red alarm ringing as someone fell ill in the shower

I remember the lady next to me in tears as she tried desperately to breastfeed

I remember the mother opposite staring longingly out of the window

I remember the pain and the routine administering of pills to numb it

I remember willing away that little red rash on your face after you had a reaction to me using that big brand lotion on you and noting then and there to use only organic and mild products on your sensitive new skin

I remember being scared to leave you alone as I attempted to use the toilet independently for that first time

I remember the hunger, that hospital food…nibbling on biscuits and longing for visiting hours where I would be brought something more appetising

I remember that little plastic crib you laid in to my left

I remember the hot May sun beaming through that window to my right

I remember watching the clock, wishing on the time to be discharged

I remember all your new born clothes swamping you

I remember so many things from those first 48 hours…but mostly, I remember loving you more than anything and feeling like I'd already known you for a lifetime.

Through your Eyes – Starseed Skye

Sometimes I look at photos of you and wonder

What it must be like to see the world through your eyes

You etheric being of pure love

When I look into your eyes, I see mysteries of times gone by, or perhaps yet to arrive

Some say we must teach you, but I think it is you who is teaching us

Born from the dark nest of the womb into this earthly realm, how must that have felt- tell me- do you remember?

The language you speak is that of the light, perhaps we go wrong in making you unlearn that other worldly code you naturally came to know

Tell me baby

What do you know?

Because I now you do know

Please show me the world through your eyes my baby

My beautiful starseed child

The depth of which you can love yourself, is the depth of which you can love another

Lioness Lovin

...and they will secretly wonder how she gets up each and every time with a smile

It's because what they cant see, is a fire inside her that is so strong

A knowing

She is led by and with love

The fiercest protection of all

And the king wants his queen to take her place upon the throne

And it is with pride that he bestows her majesty when she is in her full power

He trusts her intuitive knowings without doubt or question

In fact

He knows that what she feels in her waters is the compass to his anchor

He loves that she is soft

But is turned on by her fierce ability to bite back when needed

She scopes the savannah tuning into the subtleties of her surroundings

then ushers him forth, to claim their land...

Loving All of You

Raising you to love *you* the best you can
Every part of you
the light and the shadows
to deconstruct societal views of how we *should* love ourselves
so that you may love yourself loudly and proudly
love others
encourage reciprocity
to keep your cup filled
so that you may love with the overspill

Forever My Darling

I look for you in the Guyanese accent of a stranger
A caramel hue, I look for you
In the perfectly manicured nails of a pensioner on the bus
In the flavour and fluffiness of the roti I am yet to learn how to make
In the trance of the waltz of a dreamy 1950s romance
My muse, I look to you, I look for you
What I wouldn't give to hold you close
I close my eyes and can still see you, feel you.
Your perfume, your scent, the softness of your cheeks
Your powdered bosom ever present
I could be a child when I was with you
I guess we've all got some growing up to do
I didn't understand back then, the importance of your daily ritual, knelt by your bedside, in conversation with God, source, self.
That was your time, you honoured it, we respected it.
I wear your bangle for comfort and sometimes for strength
You sowed seeds that will continue to blossom forever more
You had real presence
You shared secrets with me that I will forever treasure
Forever my daring, forever my muse

When they die

What if when they die, like seeds we place them back into the earth to enrich it and plant roots for our ancestral trees.

Swaying Penguins

Swaying penguins
Holding hands
Under the stars
To me you are a melody
Together we sway in perfect synergy
Friend for life, you're stuck with me
The yin to my yang
The black to my white
Monochrome
Never monotone
All kinds of harmony
Antarctic infinity
As cold as ice
The love runs deep
As long as I sway with you, promise you'll sway with me
Swaying penguins
Holding hands
Under the stars
To me you are a melody
I was always whole but somehow you're the other half of me
Swaying penguins
Holding hands
Under the stars
To me you are a melody
Together we sway in perfect synergy
Together we sway in perfect synergy
Friends for life cos I got you, and you got me

I miss you most

I miss you most when I hear of home
A faint scent of jasmine in the breeze
Bountiful gardens take me back to summer days observing you as you tended to your lot
Sprinklers immersing each leaf with love
Dhal puri, roti, curry, fried rice
The clink and jangle of your gold bangles
When I need advice and a loving embrace without agenda
Anytime I'm south of the river with nobody to see
These are just some of the times I wish you were still here with me

You are a divine fractal of the infinite everlasting love, that is God

Through the Eyes of a Bebe – Rebirth

The first separation I ever felt was that from the tree of life within my mother's womb
Severed from the chord which fed me the elixir of life
The pathway of love between her and I
Exchanges that built an unspoken bond that can never be broken
As I exited the darkness of her womb
And was born into this earthly realm
I imagine my eyes were wide with anticipation of what I might find
My arms wide open
As was my heart
Trusting that I would be held and loved and nurtured by my earthly guardians
My innate instincts there to keep me safe somewhat
But trust was the language I held onto
Trust that the cries would be the cues that would provide all I required
The world has shown me love but sadly too it has shown me inversions
It has shown betrayal
I have betrayed
It has sought to steer me away from my soul
Cloaked me in layers that I thought I wanted
Today I say take it away
Strip me
I want to be naked
Naked as the day I was born
I do not care how that makes you feel
All I know is I want to return home
To my truest soul
To those bright eyes that see life with anticipation
With a heart wide open
Trust that hasn't been broken
To a place where there is no separation
To that place of deep knowing
That, is the place that I know will feel most like what we refer here to as
"home"

What Is Love

It's that overwhelming burst when a mother first lays eyes on her child

expressed through tears that carry the signature codes of generations

it's that grip in the heat of that moment of passion where nothing else matters but then

it's the roar of thunder as the heavens open and water streams through unbound

it's the rainbow that appears thereafter, the bright promise over all of the land

it's sacred rage when you feel betrayed, and you just want to tear it all down

it's the continuous beat of your heart every day without prompting and you stopping to give it thanks

it's forgiving yourself and forgiving the other and being happy to see them at peace

it's laughing and crying in the very same moment and feeling divine ecstasy

it's the rising of the tides and the setting of the sun and how it happens cyclically

it's a multitude of miniscule and humungous things

that is what love is to me

Dance with Nature

As I rest my feet upon your shoulders

You lift me up

Raising me to higher heights

Spinning every day but yet I never get dizzy

This existence is the epitome of my essence

Your frequency sends me into a trance

The beat of my drum is the beat of your heart

Lighting me up illuminating my path

A beautiful rhythm

It's sacred medicine every time that we dance

Ley Lines

As I ley upon your ley lines

Feeling like the world is mine

Divine energy enters me

And we dance in beautiful ecstasy

Synergy

Shhhh

Can you feel that gentle breeze

I close my eyes so that I can truly see

All the magic that's surrounding me

Anchoring in the light that emanate from every part of me

A magical exchange that has the ability to change the trajectory of humanity

As I do my part

And you play your position

Ley lines

Connecting dots

Lighting the grid

Forever

The Man in The Chapel at the top of the Tor

He thanked me and as we parted ways, rather than goodbye, he said this…

"Until the infinite and beyond"

The Bridge

Sometimes I can't stand you

I watch you from afar and see the potential pitfalls

But if I am the child of the Most High, how can I watch you fall?

I cannot

He told me that I must abide by love

And so I stretch out my hand to help light your path

A bridge over troubled waters, I lay my shield down

Guided by my true heart

Led by love

Love knows no bounds and separation from that which is love, is merely an illusion.

Crowned/Halo

I see you
Crowned in all your glory
I see your coils as they salute to the sun
One by one
Spirals of love
Rooted in majesty
Right to the very tip
Sometimes braided
Each symmetrical row bound with love
Sometimes locks that hang free
A conduit for Jah's divine energy
I love it most when it's wild and free
Your coils loving on each other as they kink and curl
Clinging to one another as they dance
Yes
Look at you
Crowned
In all your glory

Past Life Love

Could it be that you were once my son, my lover, my father or my brother?

Dancing with sun

Every day we do our dance I stare into his eyes and he showers me with love

Every single strand of DNA is activated, and I know that this is real

Pouring high vibrations into every single cell

Consistency is key and yes, he rises *every* day

And I show him I am grateful in my own unique and special way

When he goes down, I am fixated with colours of ecstasy

Floating on a natural high as I give him all of me

When we combine our energies two unite as one

Every single day is love when I'm dancing with the sun

To My King

To my king from another lifetime
Thank you for showing yourself to me
For reminding me where this burning love and passion inside resides
Cracking open my heart to all that I know I deserve and truly desire
Thank you for showing me that you were my lion and I your lioness
That we ruled with love and power
You've been calling me for quite some time
And when I showed you I was ready
You revealed yourself and our epic love story fully
Perhaps losing you is why I have a birthmark right at the place of my heart
But in finding you again I know that every little thing is gonna be more than alright
I love you to infinity
Your lioness
Your Queen
Katrina

For the Divine Masculine

I understand that society has skewed what it is to embody your essence

I see you stepping into this new way of being and it is beautiful.

As I rise in my feminine power, just know that I will always hold a space for you

So do not fall for me, rather, take your ascent to meet me where I am at and let us soar to higher heights, together.

Lotus

Just like a lotus blossoms from the depths of the mud

so does the divine feminine

full of wisdom and beauty as she blooms upon the surface of the water

her essence is to be admired from afar as the moonlight highlights her love.

Ritual

What is a ritual? To me, it is the habitual practice of self-love.

I am
I am peace
I am power
I am truth
I am love

Back to Shore
And soon enough you'll become the observer
You will learn to watch your thoughts and feelings
Come
And go
Like waves do as they meet the shore
You will learn to tread the water
And then again
You will let out a deep exhale when you feel the land beneath your feet as you are reunited
With the sand…

A letter to my daughters

And to my darling girls, if they ask you to jump, don't respond with "how high?"

You stand up tall and ask they "why?"

Comfort zones have invisible barriers perfectly designed for you to break. Don't be afraid to use your voice, even when it shakes.

And if they try to make you follow the status quo, sometimes you will have to go toe to toe.

If I can give you one piece of advice to take on your way

Let your intuition guide you, it always knows the best way.

Mumma

A Dream Come True

I saw you on the vision board of my dreams
and when the universe conspired to manifest you into reality
It was then that I knew the power of love

Sisterhood
Sometimes the lights that shine brightest need their candle reignited by the flame of another too.

Comparison

Mother nature does not compare herself to you she just blooms

Two Different Trees

stop looking outside
come home
to self
Comparing you to me, would be like comparing the flowers from
two completely different trees

The cure for comparison

A first I ignored the symptoms
But as they grew with intensity
I could no longer supress the sharp sudden grip they had on me
Her family seemed happier than mine
Her content more banging
Her 'look' more put together
I went back to me
Back to her
Self-doubt
Belittlement
Discouragement
At an all-time high
The definition?
Well today I was diagnosed
As he asked me to describe my symptoms, I reeled them off one by one
Unable to provide a prescription for the cause, I took myself off frantically searching the internet for a prognosis
Tab after tab
Back and forth until the lightbulb switched on – the line-
Switch off to tune in
Back home
Back to me

Roots Run Deep

When it came for the day her to be removed
I stood and watched in both awe and anger
Man and his machinery versus mother nature
As he fought against her roots, sweat beading on his brow
I smiled

He hadn't bargained for her strength
It reminded me much of my ancestral history
For years our heritage torn down by white patriarchy
But we, the decedents still here
Remembering
Unlearning to relearn
Rising from the seeds and rich soil in which we were planted
Proof of our power
Planted within the melanin in our skin
DNA doesn't lie
The lands from whence we came
Bountiful
Rich
The western world built on the back of our inheritance
Our majesty reflected in everything you enjoy today

New Earth - The Fork in the Road
Worlds apart
Torn between two paradigms
Old and new
Which way to go
Don't ask me
You choose

Trust
If I leap, will you catch me?
I ask the universe
If you have to ask, we still have some work to do
It replies

Tapestry

In the majestic tapestry of life, everything happens by design

Mother Nurture

What the outdoors means to me?

The unwavering love of a mother

It doesn't matter night or day, she's there

A place to hold and hide my secret tears

When I run, she is there, no judgement

No questions

When I am depleted, she charges me

As I rest my bare feet softly into the grass

Each blade wraps my feet in love

Invisible electrons sent into my aura

Dance

When I dance, I close my eyes and feel the tempo of the music

And it that moment

It is more than just dancing

It is a silent acknowledgement of the fact that I miss my grandparents

Of pride in my heritage

Of memories of moments gone by

Of the opportunity to share joy and movement with my daughters

As we bump hips, my mind privately transports me to memories of watching my mum do the same with her mum all those years ago

I look at my babies as they bop and bounce and momentarily wonder if they'll remember these times and perhaps do the same with their children

Yes

The moments of movement are more than just dancing

They are the thread which weaves together both past and present

Grass

A blade of grass will grow wherever there is soil no matter how many times you cut her down

At One

At one with nature
At one with self
At one with source

Patience

you want spoiler alerts when they talk of your favourite box set
yet you want to skip certain chapters of your life just to see how the story ends
be patient my love
have trust and let it unfold
naturally

Be wary of those who only wish to wallow with you in your grief but don't want to dance with you in your glory.

Truth
I would rather I tell you the ugly truth than a beautiful lie.

The Little Old Lady With the Pretty Front Garden

I watched from the window as the coffin bearers lifted her cautiously into the hearse. I never knew the little old lady with the with the pretty front garden, but I used to watch from my kitchen window as she'd take out her rubbish or tend to her flowers. When I saw the light shining through her net curtains, I felt comforted.

Every springtime her front lawn would blossom with daffodils and tulips. That pop of colour each year was reassurance.
I often wondered if she has someone to take care of her. I felt sure she did, the occasional car parked on her driveway gave indication of that.

One day she left her home for the last time, I watched people gathered at the roadside and wondered, were they family, were they friends, how did they feel? I mean, it was none of my business, but I cared.

Soon thereafter, a "For Sale" sign appeared pitched in the front garden. It was no longer pretty. It's amazing how a person's spirit leaves with them when they go. A home, with a pretty front garden, now a lifeless shell.

The "For Sale" sign was swiftly replaced with a "Sold" sign, I watched from my kitchen window as a new family moved in. They appeared celebratory; did they know anything of the little old lady I wondered? Perhaps not, perhaps they didn't care. I wonder if the front garden will bloom the same way next spring...just a thought.

7th of November

Many people have asked me what triggered my awakening, to be honest there have been many moments.
You'll find when you look back on your experiences to date, some will stand out as shifting your reality from that moment, forever.

One of those was 7th November. The day I received the call from my brother that changed my literally shattered my heart. I had noticed that our usually settled baby had the most unusually unsettled sleep from the early hours of the morning. It is said that babies have heightened intuition, in hindsight, I know why.

Against the wishes of my loved ones and against my better judgement, I jumped in my car to cross London. In a state of shock, I had a collision, parked up and jumped on a train at a station I couldn't name until days later.

When I arrived at Wimbledon, I physically had to brace myself for quite some time, just to carry out the simple action of opening a door. On the other side of the door were two women who mean the world to me, one of them here in body but no longer alive.

My nan looked so peaceful I honestly thought she would wake up. As a short while passed and we watched such an important part of our family being carried away, it was surreal. To come face to face with what occurs with the finality of life.

That year was a traumatic one, life went on as normal as possible, we had no choice but for it to. The world keep turning and whilst you are beset with grief and wish it would stop, in other places, new life has just begun and there is joy. Whilst life keeps moving and you slowly re-emerge from the depths of grief, it is beset with a sense of guilt. Then you move through the realisation that of course, it has to, life is a God given gift after all. The juxtaposition of heart wrenching pain versus heart warming memories comes like waves and it is especially hard to watch to watch your nearest and dearest in their grief.

But with time, you learn to ride those waves. Sometimes they have you in their grip, it's all engulfing and it takes the wind out of your sails, and other times you surf them like a pro. Then one day, the grief turns into gratitude for the life and times that you were able to share. Slowly you will dance and laugh again. You will begin to notice the little things that light you up once more. Your eyes will appear brighter, but with a perspective that is forever changed.

Your legacy taught me the importance of love.

In closing…

I have experienced many divine and life altering moments.

Each has led me from season to season, sometimes with a smooth transition, other times, with a bit of a bump.

It is said that hindsight is 20/20 vision, it gives you clarity that you might not, or could not possibly have had in the moments preceding.

Often, you will find when you look back on your life, that every single thing was destined to occur to lead you to this very moment. When you find acceptance and gratitude for it all through your own healing and sharing your light, it becomes so much easier to navigate, especially if you know your own soul chose this all, as part of your own evolution.

I believe, or know, that every single interaction, encounter or experience I have had, was pre- ordained. As it says in the bible "Before I formed you in the womb, I knew you"- Jeremiah 1:5.

As I write this last piece of the book, I am in Giza, Egypt, a sacred site bursting with electromagnetic energy and steeped in history. A beautiful stargate that I was destined to come and anchor in and with.

It has felt like the perfect place to set my intentions and compass for my personal new solar sail around the sun. Being very intentional with the words I use, I continue to affirm that my journey in Egypt has not been a trip, because the word trip would imply it was by accident or a fall.

It was during a chat with a wise man in Cairo whose original intentions for a tourist such as myself, would be to sell me cold-pressed aromatherapy oils, that things took a turn and provided divine confirmation. As these things do when kindred souls align.

Our interaction was more than I could have foreseen when I first entered his premises. The conversation went on from me commenting on the aroma of various potent oils, to us having an hour-long discussion about chakras, the Sirius gateway, Orion's Belt, blue lotus and other precious plants. From there it went onto the power of frequency and sound, the 365 senses, season and cycles of life. Thereafter taking a journey into the magnetic poles of the earth, healing energy, crystals and so much more!

What was beautiful in that fated encounter, was that it aligned with everything I had set my prior intentions for whilst travelling in Egypt.

What stood out amongst it all was his very deliberate intent to ensure that I left the place enlightened with the distinct difference between Egyptology and Kemetology.

In that moment I know I was being handed a key. It was the look he gave me and the gestures he made as doing so which seeded a very clear message. He taught me that Kemet means "black land" and that it was a matriarchal society. Which is very poignant and rings true to the return of what we are seeing unfold before our very eyes at this time.

As life would have it, offering full circles along the way. I started this book saying that sometimes, it is through the lens of another, that you are reminded of who you are. That occurred again when before departing, he told me this "there are some things we will not know, but you are a channel, you don't need a tour guide, guide yourself".

So, whilst adventuring on this journey we know as life, learn to lean into and trust the divine detours and yes you may have teachers, healers and people you admire, but none other than your own soul can take you to your North Star.

With love and gratitude,

Katrina

Website: www.unrefinedsoul.com

Instagram: @theunrefinedsoulscribe

Printed in Poland
by Amazon Fulfillment
Poland Sp. z o.o., Wrocław

32092759R00174